WISDOM
AND THE
BOOK
OF
PROVERBS

WISDOM
AND THE
BOOK
OF
PROVERBS

A Hebrew Goddess Redefined

BERNHARD LANG

THE PILGRIM PRESS
New York

Biblical quotations marked RSV *are from the* Revised Standard
Version of the Bible, *copyright 1946, 1952 and © 1971, 1973 by*
the Division of Christian Education, National Council of Churches,
and are used by permission. Acknowledgment of permission to
reproduce illustrations is made on page 177.

Library of Congress Cataloging-in-Publication Data

Lang, Bernhard, 1946–
   Wisdom and the Book of Proverbs.
   Based on the author's thesis (Th.D.—Eberhard-Karls-
Universität, Tübingen, 1975) published under title:
Frau Weisheit.
   Bibliography: p. 179.
   1. Bible. O.T. Proverbs I–IX—Criticism, interpreta-
tion, etc. 2. Wisdom (Biblical character) 3. Wisdom—
Biblical teaching. I. Lang, Bernhard, 1946–
Frau Weisheit. II. Title.
BS1465.2.L36   1986   223'.706   85-21527
ISBN 0-8298-0568-0 (pbk.)

The Pilgrim Press, 132 West 31 Street, New York, NY 10001

For
C. McD. and J.F.H.

CONTENTS

PREFACE

Like any other academic piece of writing, this book has a long story, and I am indebted to many who have helped along the way. A first draft of one section was presented to the *Ecole biblique* of Jerusalem in 1971 as an *élève titulaire* thesis. A draft of the whole book was accepted by the Faculty of Catholic Theology in the Eberhard-Karls-Universität of Tübingen, Germany, as a Th.D. thesis in 1975. My esteemed doctor-father was Dr. Herbert Haag, and Dr. Hans Peter Rüger of the Protestant faculty served as a referee. The thesis has subsequently been published, in German, as *Frau Weisheit: Deutung einer biblischen Gestalt* (Düsseldorf: Patmos, 1975).

Three eminent scholars have helped me to clarify and structure my thoughts on the Wisdom poems studied in this book. Hans Peter Rüger of Tübingen prevented me from falling into many linguistic traps when I prepared the original thesis. Dr. Hellmut Brunner taught me the rudiments of Egyptian language and guided me through ancient instruction texts in his Tübingen seminars. Finally, Dr. Morton Smith of Columbia University, New York, enabled me to break away from certain textbook misconceptions about the development of ancient Israelite religion and come to my own conclusions about how the original Israelite paganism eventually gave way to monotheistic Judaism.

My doctor-father encouraged me not to be shy of expressing unpopular views and defending ideas not (yet) shared by the guild of biblical and religious scholars.

The Pilgrim Press gave me the opportunity to reconsider my

somewhat dusty thesis in the light of recent research and, especially, my own *Monotheism and the Prophetic Minority: An Essay in Biblical History and Sociology* (Sheffield: Almond, 1983). Thus the present book is a fairly thorough revision of *Frau Weisheit* made during the winter of 1984-85, when I taught at the Gutenberg-Universität of Mainz, Germany. The new version reflects a much more radical approach than the one advocated in the original thesis. Therefore, I must ask colleagues to quote from the present book rather than to rely on *Frau Weisheit*.

I am especially grateful to Dr. Reinhard Ulrich for his careful translation of my original work, which I used as the basis of this English revised edition, as well as for the editorial assistance of Stephanie Kirkman.

I dedicate this book to Dr. Colleen McDannell and Dr. John F. Hurdle, two friends who have helped a German *Ordinarius* not to remain sitting on his academic chair or in the library of his home university, but to explore American libraries as well—and to enjoy their inspiring company.

ABBREVIATIONS OF BOOKS AND PERIODICAL LITERATURE

AJSL *American Journal of Semitic Languages and Literatures*
ANEP *The Ancient Near East in Pictures Relating to the Old Testament,* edited by James B. Pritchard, 2d ed. Princeton, NJ: Princeton University Press, 1969.
ANET *Ancient Near Eastern Texts Relating to the Old Testament,* edited by James B. Pritchard, 3d ed. Princeton, NJ: Princeton University Press, 1969.
AOAT *Alter Orient und Altes Testament*
ASTI *Annual of the Swedish Theological Institute*
BA *Biblical Archaeologist*
BASOR *Bulletin of the American Schools of Oriental Research*
BHS *Biblia Hebraica Stuttgartensia*
BZ *Biblische Zeitschrift*
BZAW *Beiheft zur Zeitschrift für die alttestamentliche Wissenschaft*
CAD *The Assyrian Dictionary of the Oriental Institute of the University of Chicago*
CBQ *Catholic Biblical Quarterly*
ET English translation/English translator
HAL *Hebräisches und aramäisches Lexikon zum Alten Testament,* edited by Walter Baumgartner et al., fasc. 1ff. Leiden: Brill, 1967ff.
HTR *Harvard Theological Review*
JANES *Journal of the Ancient Near Eastern Society of Columbia University*

JBL	*Journal of Biblical Literature*
JJS	*Journal of Jewish Studies*
JPS	*The Writings.* A new translation of the Holy Scriptures, edited by the Jewish Publication Society. Philadelphia: Jewish Publication Society, 1982.
JQR	*Jewish Quarterly Review*
Mansi	*Sacrorum conciliorum nova et amplissima collectio,* edited by J. D. Mansi
NAB	*New American Bible*
NEB	*New English Bible*
PEQ	*Palestine Exploration Quarterly*
PG	*Patrologiae cursus completus, series graeca,* edited by J. P. Migne
RB	*Revue Biblique*
RHPhR	*Revue d'Histoire et de Philosophie religieuses*
RHR	*Revue de l'Histoire des Religions*
RSV	*Revised Standard Version of the Bible*
SEÅ	*Svensk Exegetisk Årsskrift*
UF	*Ugarit-Forschungen*
VT	*Vetus Testamentum*
VTS	Supplements to *Vetus Testamentum*
ZA	*Zeitschrift für Assyriologie*
ZÄS	*Zeitschrift für ägyptische Sprache und Altertumskunde*
ZAW	*Zeitschrift für die alttestamentliche Wissenschaft*
ZDPV	*Zeitschrift des Deutschen Palästina-Vereins*

WISDOM
AND THE
BOOK
OF
PROVERBS

CHAPTER 1

Introduction: Wisdom, Polytheism, and the Hebrew School

The meadows mourn for the old hollowing life;
Vainly we search the earth of gods bereft;
Where once the warm and living shapes were rife
Shadows alone are left!

—FRIEDRICH SCHILLER[1]

The sages had a kind of female patron deity of whom they sometimes spoke; Hebrew tradition calls her "Wisdom." For Israel's sages, this figure was perhaps a mere personification. Some of her features, however, clearly betray her former divine nature.

—HERMANN GUNKEL[2]

The biblical book of Proverbs is an almost random collection of brief didactic discourses, poems, learned and pious sayings. Although often sophisticated and subtle in expression, most of these texts are straightforward, and their moralizing message is easy to understand. For this reason the book of Proverbs became a favorite biblical text for many Christians and Jews in both Europe and America.

The book includes, however, three poems that are "com-

3

pletely isolated: They seem to stand like erratic blocks on their own, unconnected with their surroundings."[3] Their meaning is obscure even to specialists who have spilled much ink and filled many printed pages to elucidate them. These poems, found in the first, eighth, and ninth chapters, feature a female figure called Wisdom, who herself addresses the readers, urging them to follow the wisdom teaching and inviting them to be her lovers. When I first studied these poems and their helpless, although learned, modern commentaries, I immediately felt that there were only two possible solutions to the enigma of Wisdom. Either we must continue to explain this figure in terms of the established view of the history of ancient Israelite and early Jewish literature and try to integrate her more fully into this framework, or we must rewrite the history of ancient Israelite literature in a way that provides a better place for the poems to fit in. I eventually decided to adopt the second approach, suggesting that there has been something fundamentally wrong with our conventional textbook views of biblical literature and religion. What started as an attempt at making sense of beautiful, yet elusive biblical poems became an exercise in reshaping fundamental categories.

At a purely literary level I argue that, contrary to common opinion, the first nine chapters of Proverbs are not a late, perhaps fourth-century preface that attempts to make the rest of the book sound more religious. These chapters are not only much older, but also form an independent work with a preface in Proverbs 1:1–7 and a conclusion that stood originally after Proverbs 9:18 but, by mistake or misunderstanding, has been transferred to Proverbs 9:7–10.

Dating biblical texts on the basis of their vocabulary and grammar is difficult and often impossible. In the case of Proverbs 1—9 specifically, late (i.e., postexilic) vocabulary is absent.[4] But this is not the only feature that points to a much earlier date than is normally assumed. The figure of Wisdom herself is decisive. Any attentive reader of the Old Testament will agree that the religion of most ancient Israelites was as polytheistic and "pagan" as any other cult practiced by neighboring peoples. The Israelites were people who worshiped their national god, Yahweh, along with a host of other gods and goddesses. Baal, El, Yahweh,

4

and Shemesh were all prominent gods, but we can name only one goddess: Astarte, who was probably also called the Queen of Heaven.[5] When seen in a polytheistic context it is hard to avoid the conclusion that Wisdom must be understood as another goddess.

In early Jewish thought Wisdom could not and did not remain a divine figure. Jewish monotheists developed an *interpretatio monotheistica* of some of their own pagan ancestors' views, just as later, Christian authors developed an elaborate *interpretatio Christiana* of Greek and Roman mythology as well as a "messianic" reading of Jewish texts. In the monotheistic climate of postexilic Judaism, traditional wisdom had to be rethought and the old wisdom texts had to be reedited in terms of new religious convictions. It was in this context that the apparently pale goddess Wisdom could be reinterpreted or redefined. For the monotheist reader, she was a purely poetic figure, a simple personification that could not endanger the true religion.

This is not to say that the reader's monotheistic bias distorted the original and "true" meaning of the poems. As modern literary criticism asserts, the meaning of literature does not, in any definitive fashion, reside *in* the text itself, but issues from the dynamic interaction of text and reader and belongs, ultimately, to the realm of reader experience. Sartre explains:

> When a literary work is produced, the creative act is only an incomplete, abstract impulse. If the author existed all on his own, he could write as much as he liked, but his work would never see the light of day as an *object,* and he would have to lay down his pen or despair. The process of writing, however, includes as a dialectic correlative the process of reading, and these two interrelated acts require two different agents. The combined efforts of author and reader bring into being the concrete and imaginary object that is the work of the mind. Art exists only for and through other people. Reading, in effect, seems to be the synthesis of a perceptive and·a creative process.[6]

The reader's mind, therefore, must not be seen as a mirror that simply reflects the text. The text always engages the reader's whole personality, his or her interests, preconceptions, ideas, experiences, religion, and world view. Even with the simplest

5

texts we engage in a kind of conversation, in a process that produces meaning. While blanks in a text, on the one hand, impede coherence, on the other, they actually function as stimuli for complex and varied acts of image-building. It follows that the more difficult the text, the greater the degree of requisite imagination or reader participation required. One may think of the text as a blueprint from which the reader, or a community of readers, constructs the edifice of meaning.

The Hebrew text of the poems has reached us in fairly good shape.[7] Yet this is certainly not the original version. The present text is overlaid with a veneer of mono-Yahwism, if not indeed monotheism, but in a few passages the polytheism of the original composition can still be glimpsed. It seems that Wisdom's mythological father, El, has been tacitly replaced by Yahweh. The very logic of monotheism requires the only god, Yahweh, to be the creator of the universe and to leave no place for El. The creator god of ancient Canaanite mythology was identified with, and in a way absorbed into, Yahweh. Equally, the "fear of the gods" became, by substitution of one word, the "fear of Yahweh." Thus polytheistic piety was redefined in monotheistic terms.

Goddess Wisdom was also redefined. How exactly we have no way of telling. Having no wish to patronize either ancient or modern monotheists, many of the modern commentators seem to have done what early Jewish monotheists must have done long before them: to reconcile a goddess, who no longer can be a goddess, with a monotheistic creed. To maintain that Wisdom somehow functions as a link between Creator and creation, God and humankind; to call her a hypostasis of the Creator's superior and inscrutable wisdom; to see in her appeals and harangues the voice of creation—all these are attempts to deal with the delicate situation, and they are more or less convincing to other monotheists. In criticizing some of the readings I take issue only with the assertion that the poems were *originally* composed with some such idea in mind. By arguing that Wisdom came to be regarded as a mere poetic personification (of school wisdom) I suggest that this was probably the earliest and most elegant redefinition of the goddess in a monotheistic context.

What kind of goddess was Wisdom? In order to answer this question we have to turn to the text of the poems. Because

6

Wisdom clearly acts as a teacher, I propose to understand her as the divine patronness of the Israelite school system. Recently, scholars have become increasingly aware of the existence as well as the significance of the ancient Israelite schools. For ancient Israel and other ancient states, scribal training was of paramount importance for the creation of administrative systems and early bureaucracies. Scribal education and "wisdom" as its key concept are crucial to our understanding of the poems.

THE ANCIENT ISRAELITE SCHOOL

According to Voltaire, the Israelites "were so far from having public schools to instruct their youth that their language did not even include a term designating such an institution." He portrayed Israel as an ignorant and barbaric nation.[8] In a similar vein, Ludwig Köhler, by trade an Old Testament scholar and not an acid-tongued philosopher, holds that "everything known as a school and as schooling has been foreign to the Hebrew people until quite late in their history."[9] This sort of judgment was meant to dispose of Nachtigal's venerable speculation, according to which there had been academies and scholarly literature in Israel before Talmudic times.[10] Ernest Renan's speculation seemed equally unfounded. For Renan, the poetry of an Isaiah presupposes some sort of training and education: "une telle perfection suppose l'école."[11] A society without schools is unlikely to produce more than mere "oral" literature. Voltaire and Köhler, however, tried to account for the biblical culture without assuming the existence of schools. While the philosopher despised the ignorance of the Hebrews, the biblical scholar romanticized their village folklife. For both of them, the Israelites were a peasant people.

Archaeologists and students of the numerous Near Eastern inscriptions written in cuneiform and hieroglyphs knew better. In 1887 Egyptian bedouins found what turned out to be part of a fourteenth-century B.C. state archive of the Amarna pharaohs. This archive included numerous letters, written in cuneiform script on clay and sent to Egypt by Palestinian city princes. "Schools and libraries," explained A. H. Sayce, "must have existed everywhere, and the art of writing and reading must have

7

Scale 1:3

Figure 1. Drawings scratched on the vertical face of the palace steps in ancient Lachish. The beginning of an alphabet is on the right-hand side. The drawings are dated circa 800 B.C. and are attributed to a schoolboy.

been as widely spread as it was in Europe before the penny post."[12] A generation later further evidence turned up. In 1924 the Berlin scholar Adolf Erman published an ancient Egyptian schoolbook. The parallels between the *Instruction of Amenemope* and certain passages in the biblical book of Proverbs were too obvious to be purely accidental.[13] It was concluded, therefore, that Israel's teachers must have attended school in foreign countries and that they brought home their books from abroad. Taking foreign literature as their model, they created Israelite school literature, part of which eventually found its way into the biblical canon.

When scribblings of an ancient Hebrew alphabet were found in the Judean town of Lachish during a British excavation in 1938, scholars began to consider the issue even more carefully and finally became convinced of the existence of an institutionalized scribal training. Here is how the British press reported the findings, taking the existence of schools for granted:

> The scribblings found on the vertical face of one of the steps of the Jewish [Judean] palace, which the expedition is beginning to excavate inside the city, were probably the work of some schoolboy. They consist of a rectangular drawing, with lines across it much after the fashion of a Union Jack, a drawing of a lion, and the first five letters of the Phoenician-Hebrew alphabet. . . . From these discoveries it seems clear that the Phoenician-Hebrew alphabet was in general use in the Kingdom of Judah and was being taught in the schools of

8

Lachish before Nebuchadnezzar carried the Jews into captivity.[14]

Now there was talk of a school for scribal training in Israel after all. It was assumed that the schools of Israel were not essentially different from the corresponding institutions of its neighbors, on which much information became available.[15] The book of Proverbs, specifically, came to be regarded as the school's literary legacy. The "wise men," occasionally mentioned in biblical texts, were now simply taken to be the teachers, professors, and literati of the scribal school. When the prophets denounced "wise men," a ready explanation was now available: Their attack was directed against teachers and scribes of the royal court. Certain sections in the book of Proverbs that are not explicitly "religious" were thought to contain the "wisdom" of such wise men and regarded as the somewhat illegal philosophy of intellectuals and politicians who, with the help of foreign thought, had emancipated themselves from traditional piety. Consequently, it was argued, a secular ideology developed among the elite class of civil servants, a mode of thought that was effectively perpetuated in the scribal school. Only later did wisdom acquire a religious character, progressively absorbing religious and moral ideas of a distinctively Israelite kind. According to one view, it was under prophetic pressure, possibly not until postexilic times, that pragmatic wisdom was made to conform to the world view of Israel's religious orthodoxy.[16] After the exile, when prophecy had run its course, wisdom quietly and soberly took on the succession, serving as the everyday philosophy of the unpolitical Jewish communities in the Diaspora.[17]

Although this view is still argued in works of most recent date, it has now given way to a different perception. Conclusions concerning the links between the neighboring cultures and Israel's school system and civil service had been reached too hastily. The book of Proverbs had become an object of too quick a search for a distinctive and otherwise unknown view of life and the world supposedly held by a select group whose philosophy was met with prophetic hostility. Research into biblical wisdom literature has not escaped the errors committed in other areas of contemporary biblical scholarship, especially in research on Is-

9

rael's law and the psalms. In each of the three fields—Law, Psalms, and Wisdom—the question of the institutional setting *(Sitz im Leben),* as urged by Hermann Gunkel, has led to dead-end conjectures. In the field of law, scholars believed that they had found a body of divine law with its attendant support structure, the sacred confederation of tribes. For the psalms, they postulated holy days that supposedly vanished at a later date and tried to reconstruct their respective rituals. In the case of wisdom literature, scholars felt that they had found the distinct conceptual world and literature of an elitist class of civil servants. In recent years, especially in the 1960s and 1970s, the climate of Old Testament scholarship has changed. The eagerness and readiness to construct hypotheses has given way to a soberer concern with the texts.

Klaus Koch, Erhard Gerstenberger, and James Barr have given basic direction to the study of wisdom in the Old Testament.[18] They have drawn attention to the fact that the mode of thinking, which has often been specifically assigned to wisdom, is by no means limited to wisdom literature. Also, Gerstenberger notes that wisdom teaching has not been confined to the school, but that similar teachings must have been current in the clan, an older and more primitive social structure. He adds that the distinction between "divine law" and "human wisdom," so familiar to us, is foreign to the Old Testament world. Barr insists that scholars were much too quick to regard orthodoxy in Israel from the perspective of narrative and prophetically interpreted history, bracketing out wisdom literature or, at best, letting it stand as the literature of those who stand on the outer edge of normative teaching. Consequently, a thorough revision of our understanding of wisdom, wisdom literature, school, and the scribal class has become necessary.

It remains indisputable that the book of Proverbs originated in the school and was being read there.[19] However, we should not think of the school as an exclusively elitist institution. Egyptian school literature strongly emphasizes career thinking. There is no such emphasis in Proverbs because Israel did not offer many career opportunities. Israel was too small a country both in area and population.[20] The Israelite or Judean scribe and civil servant was much less influential than his Egyptian or Mesopota-

10

mian colleague. Therefore, he plays almost no part in biblical literature. "Here two factors are to be reckoned with," explains Morton Smith:

> First, the petty courts could hardly support much in the way of a secretariat, just as they could not afford very large priestly bodies. Second, and more important, writing was alphabetic and therefore required little special training. Consequently, while of course we find a "secretary" and a "recorder" or two mentioned as high officials in the courts from David's time on, we have no reason to suppose that they were members of a special "scribal class" or that they had any peculiar training not possessed by the other equally literate members of the court. It is a priori likely that as books increased there came to be trained calligraphers who made a living by copying them, and who may have eked out their income by teaching writing and perhaps reading and occasionally something about the content of some of the books they copied. But there is no reason to suppose that such petty craftsmen and elementary teachers should be equated with the high officials of the court. At most some of them may have been employed about the court as copyists to keep well-written records and produce well-written documents—a sort of stenographic staff. This is quite a different thing from the scribal classes of Mesopotamia and Egypt—definite groups of highly-trained individuals who had mastered the complicated arts of writing in demotic, hieratic, hieroglyphic, and cuneiform, and who consequently monopolized the positions requiring literacy in the great courts (except insofar as Aramaic was used in Mesopotamia). In Israel we should suppose that, although some teachers of reading and writing did put together collections of commonplace sayings as practice books for their students (the sort of thing represented in this country by *McGuffey's Fifth Reader*) there was never any important "scribal class."[21]

Morton Smith is certainly quite correct in saying that an important and influential scribal class did not exist during the time of the Israelite and Judean monarchies. Yet he may be mistaken in making the teachers and scribes look very much like the poor Torah scroll copyists, known to tourists from their dark, narrow, and windowless stores in Jerusalem's Meah Shearim. Despite the

11

popular recognition of Torah writing as an honored and expert profession, the scribe, who also may be an elementary-school teacher, barely makes a living. Smith may also be too quick in following Albright's assertion that "the twenty-two-letter alphabet could be learned in a day or two by a bright student and in a week or two by the dullest."[22] Training a scribe properly must certainly have taken several months, if not several years. Although we have to be aware of Morton Smith's warning not to confuse Israel's institutions with those of its politically more important and bureaucratically more developed neighbors, we should assume the existence of schools and scribal training in biblical Israel. Such institutions were small but certainly not as unproductive in the proliferation of literature as Smith would have one believe. The Wisdom poems are of much too good a quality for this to be true.

What Is Wisdom?

The assumption that there was a distinctive way of thinking, exclusively associated with wisdom literature, is in even greater need of revision than our understanding of school and bureaucratic elite. The school literature shows no evidence of an isolated, peculiar way of thinking that might have been in fundamental opposition to the message of the prophets. The book of Proverbs does not contain secular or antireligious elements that could be traced to an "enlightened," secularly oriented class of civil servants and court officials. The prophets had no cause to denounce a "sapiential world view" as godless or heretical. There was no such thing as a nonreligious school literature, nor was there anything like a "sapiential world view" that was fundamentally different from the thinking of other social groups. In fact, in school literature, the national-religious traditions of Israel do not play a part. God's activity is seen, not in the fate of the nation, but in the destiny of individuals and in the order of creation. All this, however, has nothing to do with an isolated view of the world but should be regarded as literary convention. That the book of Proverbs omits the specific elements of Israelite history—national feeling, the patriarchal and Exodus traditions, prophetic preaching, and so on—does not imply that the authors

12

and readers of Proverbs were living in a world of their own, a world without history. It is simply wrong to be looking in the book of Proverbs for a complete image of the authors' world and society and to regard it as the sole reading material of its consumers. Consequently, it is impossible to discern a distinct view of religion or of history specifically reserved for "wisdom." This also applies to the conception of a divine world order, so clearly displayed in Proverbs, that humans can comprehend and whose wrath they feel whenever they fail to submit to its logic. The concept of world order may not be set apart as a specifically and exclusively sapiential idea either. Here, we simply have an exceptionally clear statement of the accepted and commonly shared world view and not, as some scholars believed, an exception to the rule of biblical thought. Wherever we look in the Bible we find "in manyfold variation, yet with total clarity, that the dominant background of Old Testament thought and faith is characterized by the idea of a comprehensive order of the world and by the belief in creation in the broadest sense of the term, a belief which, in many of its aspects, Israel shares with her neighbors."[23]

The Hebrew term *ḥokmah,* usually rendered as "wisdom," may be used to indicate the educational climate of the Israelite school. In English we distinguish between a "smart guy" and a wise, experienced person. On the one hand, we recognize a "smart guy" for superior abilities in dealing with practical, everyday problems. He or she is quick to react correctly at the appropriate time and knows how to deal with people. Yet we do not value just being smart too highly. On the other hand we count wisdom, the quality of a mature personality, among our highest values. Wisdom, according to the philosopher Kant, is "reason, matured through experience."[24] Schiller jokingly juxtaposed the two kinds of wisdom in a little poem:

Wisdom

To some she is the goddess great;
To some the milk-cow of the field—
Their worship is to calculate
The butter she will yield.[25]

The Israelite, however, makes no distinction between smart and wise. *Hokmah* denotes both wisdom proper and smartness; both concepts have equal value. A case in point is the famed wisdom of King Solomon, illustrated by an anecdote that, at best, may stand as an example of cunning intelligence: the king exposing the woman's false testimony with a rather cruel hoax.[26] Another dimension of wisdom can be seen in the prophet Isaiah's assertion that "Yahweh is wise," with the implication that Israel's god is wily and capable of playing tricks on the enemy.[27]

In addition to smartness and wisdom, *hokmah* refers to technical skill, the knowledge and ability needed to carry out a particular activity. The practical craftsmanship of artisans and builders, the intuitive technique of the sailor, the cleverness of the merchant, the finesse of the diplomat, the keen eye of the navigator, even the Machiavellianism of the man in power: all this can be referred to as wisdom.[28] Wisdom is needed in dealing with material objects as well as with human beings. It is worth noting that not only the Hebrew term, but also the Greek *(sophia)* and the Middle High German *(wîsheit)* use a single term to denote the meaning of practical, mechanical skill as well as intellectual ability. Thus *wîsheit* does not only mean knowledge based on experience, the ability to counsel and make judgments, courtly manners, and rhetorical skill, but also mastery in the crafts.[29] Wisdom means competence.

Wisdom, then, has many facets, resembling an elusive virtue the Greeks called *mētis*. A recent study of this term describes it as

> a type of intelligence, a way of thinking, a mode of knowing; it implies a complex but very coherent whole of mental attitudes, of intellectual behaviors which combine flair, wisdom, foresight, flexibility of the mind, dissimulation, watchful attention, a sense of opportunity, varied skills, an experience acquired over time; it applies to transient, mobile, disconcerting and ambiguous realities which do not lend themselves to precise measurement, nor to exact calculation, nor to rigorous reasoning.[30]

Lacking the Greek *mētis* or the Hebrew *hokmah*, no one is able to cope with the complexities of life.

In the school literature a wise or smart person is one who is open-minded, willing to learn, disciplined, and therefore an

14

ultimately successful student. Accordingly, wisdom is not innate, but must be acquired through learning. In the process of communicating wisdom the teacher does not make allowances for individual characteristics or childhood needs. The teacher acts according to the maxim "Train up a youth in the way he [or she] ought to go [in later life] [Prov. 22:6]."[31] Anyone who, with the help of parents and teachers, professional and social experience, has striven for and acquired knowledge and moral discipline is to be counted among the wise. The opposite of a wise person is a *peti*, an immature youth. (*Peti* should not be rendered as "simpleminded person," following modern Hebrew usage. It means instead "young person," like the cognate Arabic *fatan*.) Initially, the young person is not wise, but inexperienced, immature, and uneducated and thus readily misled into wickedness and evil. The young man (women are largely outside the biblical teachers' concern and therefore ignored) may all-too-easily become a bad person, perhaps even an incorrigible good-for-nothing, ne'er-do-well, and mischief-maker. A *peti* may turn out to be either a wise person or a good-for-nothing, a *leṣ*. (Here again, the traditional translation as "scoffer" is incorrect.) In the book of Proverbs the *leṣ* is a good-for-nothing or a ne'er-do-well, the incorrigible, stubborn, and wicked person who would not think of subjecting to the authority of a teacher for the sake of acquiring wisdom. He is a constant mischief-maker who delights in mischief-making.[32] Incorrigibly wicked and altogether wise persons are rare human types; one comes across them more often as pedagogic fictions than one does in reality. Teachers, however, should be allowed to simplify the complex real world into clear contrasts and to draw for their students a straightforward picture of the ideal, using black and white. The ideal, toward which the teachers are working, is quite conservative—students are to conform to the given order of their world and society. Anyone who dares to oppose this order causes his or her own nemesis.

The first nine chapters of the book of Proverbs have their origin in this educational climate. We are not dealing here with a consciously contructed literary work, but just a collection of didactic poetry, a collection of brief discourses and poems for use in teaching, a reading text that serves as a source book for teachers. The teachers did not have to follow a prescribed sequence. No passage presupposes another. Some parts are almost identical in content and may be exchanged readily. Apparently, it has been left to the teacher's discretion how to organize the material in actual classroom use. What one is faced with today, then, is far from being a topically arranged, systematically constructed essay or textbook, moving from easier to more difficult subject matter. It is only natural that such a collection of texts, or even their arrangement, does not have to be the work of a single author. A collection of this kind can easily be enlarged, corrected, rearranged, and abridged as need or inclination dictates. These characteristics of the text as a compilation of materials, however, make it quite difficult to demonstrate whatever reediting and changing may have taken place and inhibit the use of the conventional methods of analyzing literary layers and editorial changes that have been successful in Pentateuch research and with some of the prophetic literature.

The poems on Wisdom are in the first, eighth, and ninth chapters of the book of Proverbs. Their poetic quality is beyond doubt, and their beauty can be appreciated still today. Standing out from the rest of Proverbs, these texts "lend a graciousness and beauty to the book as a whole which without them would seem barren and utilitarian enough," writes the author and literary critic Mary Ellen Chase:

> Some wiser men must have composed them, poets of imagination and larger understanding. . . . Here are Job and the best of the Psalms; here are thought and vision which make the rest of the book of Proverbs barren and almost futile. The monotonous style of most of its chapters is here relieved by stateliness, dignity, and grace; and the conception of wisdom as that power before the creation of the world, "set up from everlasting," reduces the drab notions of the other sages to dust and ashes.[33]

"After such satisfaction as this," concludes the critic, "it seems unnecessary and redundant to comment further on the book of Proverbs."

PART ONE
WISDOM AS TEACHER
(Proverbs 1:20–33)

The Poem Proverbs 1:20–33

20 *[Lady*] Wisdom chants on the street,*
In the square she raises her voice,
21 At the top of the busy street *(?) she cries out,*
At the entrance of the city gate she speaks:
22 *"How long, immature ones, will you love immaturity?*
[Will] mischief-makers delight in mischief-making
And fools hate knowledge?
23 *Give heed to my admonition!*
Yes, I will speak my mind to you,
I will make known my lesson to you.
24 *Because I speak, and you refuse [to listen],*
I lift my hand [in warning], and no one heeds,
25 *And you would have none of my advice,*
Ignoring all my teaching,
26 *Therefore I will laugh out loud at your calamity,*
I will mock, when panic strikes you,
27 *When panic strikes you like a whirlwind,*
When distress and anguish come upon you.
28 *Then they will call upon me, but I will not answer;*
They will seek me, but will not find me.
29 *Since they hate knowledge*

*The term Lady Wisdom, used only occasionally in this book, is meant to be an honorific title to denote a female person of rank.

19

> And do not love the fear of Yahweh [originally: fear of
> the gods?],
> 30 Would have none of my advice,
> And reject all of my teaching,
> 31 Therefore they shall eat the fruit of their [wicked] way,
> And be sated with [the fruit of] their own devices.
> 32 For the immature kill themselves by their disobedience,
> The stubbornness of fools destroys them—
> 33 But he who listens to me will dwell secure
> And will be spared panic and terror."

The passage immediately preceding the one quoted is a pedagogic speech about wisdom, a lesson for students prepared by
their teacher, who tells them to stay away from sinners and their
wicked ways (Proverbs 1:8–19). In Proverbs 1:20 topic and literary form change. The lesson is followed by a poem in which the
teacher no longer addresses the students. Here we do not read
about wisdom or merely discuss sapiential views of life, but listen
to Wisdom herself. Wisdom, presented as a person, assumes the
teacher's role. The previous lesson dealing with the students'
behavior toward other human beings is replaced by a basic
discourse about student attitudes toward wisdom or knowledge,
Wisdom herself being the speaker. Wisdom personally deigns to
tell the students what will happen to the obstinate among them
who refuse to listen. Unlike the previous lesson, her presentation is aimed primarily at classroom behavior and not at behavior
outside of school. Using threats and intimidations, she tries to
get students to cooperate, to learn willingly, and to come to their
senses. Thus the topic of the lesson is learning and the obstinate
student—a perennial theme of pedagogy. Contemporary colleagues of the ancient Israelite teacher talk about this in terms of
lacking motivation and motivating students. Of course they are
talking about the same problem.

Before I can offer the results of our close reading of the poem
as well as justify the translation, we will take a look at two
problems that demand a more thorough investigation. We will
study the meaning of the city gate area in which Wisdom—
unexpectedly, at least to us—makes her appearance. We will see

20

that the open space about the city gate is the area where ancient Israelites would expect teachers to sit with their classes. We will further demonstrate that the very *vocabulary and speech forms* used in the poem reflect the language spoken in a classroom setting.

CHAPTER 3

Street, Square, Gate: The Setting of the Wisdom Speeches

Why does Wisdom happen to appear in the street, in the squares, at the city gate, and not elsewhere? The setting of the speech is no accident, but has almost certainly been chosen intentionally. It recurs in the introductions of the two other Wisdom poems.[1] It is therefore helpful to learn from the Old Testament and its world what connotations the terms street, square, and city gate would have had for poet and reader alike, so that we are able to answer the question why Wisdom appears in the street, in the square, and at the city gate.

The term *ḥuṣ* designates a narrow street or alley in the city. There are so many of these narrow streets in Jerusalem that the phrase "the (narrow) streets of Jerusalem" has turned into an idiom.[2] The streets are thronged with people and animals.[3] Children, too, are playing there.[4] Stores are so common in these streets that *ḥuṣot* may also mean store.[5] In times of crisis, loud laments are heard in the street.[6] People are shouting there.[7] Starving beggars are found there.[8] A blind man is coming, and people are shouting, "Away, away, touch not!"[9] Jeremiah is told to communicate his oracles "in the streets of Jerusalem."[10] The streets are proverbially covered with mire and dirt.[11] Some expressions indicate that the street functioned as a symbol for

22

public life. The outcast has no name in the street; he or she is unknown and ignored.[12] It is the place where victory or defeat is made known in times of war.[13] Right in the street—hence not secretly in a corner—pagan rituals are performed.[14] All this gives the impression of the narrow, busy, and dirty bazaar streets in the cities of the Middle East, such as Old Jerusalem, Old Cairo, and Old Damascus.

Our second term, $r^eh\!ob$, denotes the open space at the city gate,[15] at the gate of the palace,[16] or in front of the temple.[17] The term corresponds to the French *place,* the Italian *piazza,* and the English *square* or *plaza.* This is where the notables gather and talk, Job having a place of honor among them.[18] Judicial proceedings and political or cultic assemblies were held there.[19] This is also the place for public recognition and public execution.[20]

Loud lamenting is heard there in times of need.[21] Travelers are waiting there for hospitable citizens.[22] When truth and justice vanish from the squares,[23] they also no longer exist in public life, commerce, trade, the administration of justice, and communication. When children, adults, and old people are to be seen in the square, we may regard their presence as a symbol of peaceful times.[24] The open square, although not necessarily in the geographical center of the city, was the center of public life, commerce, jurisdiction, and politics. The epitome of public life as such, however, was not the open square, but the adjoining city gate.

The city gate *(sha°ar)* was one of the most important buildings of the ancient Israelite city. The Hebrew word for gate, symbolically and as *pars pro toto,* often stands for the whole city.[25] Archaeologists have unearthed a number of city gates dating from the Israelite and Judean monarchies, for instance, in Gezer, Megiddo, Beersheba, and Dan. They are relatively small buildings with thick walls, a narrow passageway of 4 meters or less, and nichelike gate chambers. The whole structure was built on a plot of around 20 × 13 meters (Beersheba) or 18 × 28 meters (Dan). The most striking feature of these buildings is that the gate chambers, which are sometimes as much as 10 meters in length, are completely open to the passageway. What is their function? "A hint may be found," explains Herzog,

23

in the benches built into some of these side rooms and from some of the installations found in them. These features indicate that the Iron Ages gates had civilian functions above and beyond their purely military-defensive objectives. In order to accommodate the civilian institutions using the gatehouse (such as the Elders of the city or Judges) as well as commercial and religious activities, these gates were designed with deep, open rooms which . . . had no military function whatsoever. The gate was defended primarily from the towers at its facade, and the gates closed off the entrance into the city from the outside only, thus leaving the side rooms open to the city even when the outer gates were locked.[26]

It should be clear, however, that the niches—in Herzog's words, "deep, open rooms"—were too small to function as a courtroom or as a place for public meetings. Both in Dan and Beersheba there was a paved, open anterior yard outside the gatehouse. This yard was enclosed by massive walls, forming part of the city's defenses. It was in these spaces of 19.5×9.4 meters (Dan) and around 20×6 meters (Beersheba) that court proceedings and council meetings could be held. In Dan, the stone benches along the side of the courtyard have actually been found. On the other, inner side of the Beersheba gatehouse there is another public square. Being 12×20 meters, it could also be used for public meetings of one kind or another.[27] In Iron Age Beersheba and Dan, then, the gatehouse no longer was a closed fortress, but an open hall dominating much open space designed for council, commerce, and ceremony. "Thus the ancient defensive gateway," comments Herzog, "was transformed during the Iron Age into the most important civilian town center, a center that was ultimately developed into the Greek *agora* and the Roman *forum*."[28]

It was in the city gate area that much of Israel's public life took place. While really large crowds, such as the four hundred prophets of 1 Kings 22:10, could only assemble and be consulted by kings Jehoshaphat and Ahab *outside* the city, where the converging tracks made a well-worn plaza, the expression "justice in/at the gate"[29] refers to the immediate area of the gatehouse. It was there that the elders and notables met. This agrees with Job's account that he went out of the city gate, sat among the notables,

24

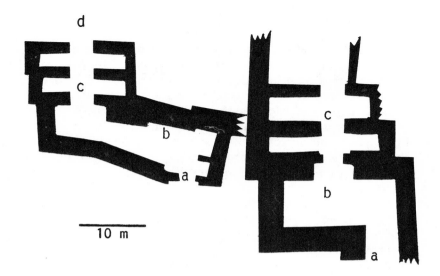

Figure 2. City gates and gatehouses in tenth-century B.C. Beersheba (left) and Dan (right). Behind the outer entrance (a) there is an open courtyard (b), the gatehouse with piers (c), and, in the case of Beersheba, an open square within the city (d).

and pronounced justice for the fatherless.[30] For the threshing floor of 1 Kings 22, where the four hundred prophets met, and for Job's role as a judge, there is a nice parallel reference in a Ugaritic epic:

> [He] raised himself up and sat at the entrance of the gate
> Beneath the trees which were by the threshing floor;
> He judged the cause of the widow,
> Tried the case of the orphan.[31]

Numerous biblical texts clearly show that the whole of public life used to take place at the gate or in the open square next to the gate. The gate was the place where legal matters were negotiated,[32] where business was done,[33] where the council of elders

25

met for political discussion,[34] yet also a place of mockery,[35] a place for all kinds of meetings,[36] and a place where the prophet found his audience.[37] The open square at the city gate should also be seen as the place where adults gathered for local self-government, which included the administration of justice.[38] "Those coming to the city gate" were the adults who had full rights as citizens and formed the political community.[39]

Women were excluded from these public, democratic institutions. The public life of gate and square, as in the Middle East to this day, was public just for men. Only rarely do we hear of women being present in the squares. Women who *are* going into the streets are looking for men.[40] The ideal wife of Proverbs 31, therefore, is found not in the street, but busy at home, while her husband is sitting at the gate with the elders. When the Kuwait Parliament was debating rights for women in 1973, the conservatives rioted "because humans of female gender have no business in the streets or in public."[41] In view of this, it is particularly noteworthy that, in our poem, *Lady* Wisdom, a *distinguished* woman, shows herself in the street.

A survey of these images of street, square, and city gate suggests that the setting of Wisdom's address is the place where a speaker may seek and find listeners. "The public does not go to the speaker," explains Lindblom,

> but the speaker has to go to his audience. A speaker must put himself in a place where people are apt to gather, or where he has a reasonable chance of collecting an audience. This kind of setting could be found at the city gate, the wall, the streets, the market squares, the sanctuaries, the roads and alleys, and the like, where people in the East used to come together, and where it was easy to get a hearing.[42]

The speaker's message was intended to affect public life. When prophet Jeremiah preached at the gates of Jerusalem he intended to set standards for public life (i.e., life at the city gate). "At all the gates of Jerusalem" he pleads for rest on the sabbath; at the Potsherd gate, the place of a Baal shrine, he speaks out against a cult he denounces as pagan.[43] This also applies to Lady Wisdom. In all three poems she advocates a kind of wisdom that is meant to apply directly to public life. Life taking place in the streets, in the market square, and at the city gate is precisely the kind of life that cannot be mastered without wisdom:

> *Wisdom is too high for a fool;*
> *in the gate he does not open his mouth.*
> —*Proverbs 24:7,* RSV

A fool has nothing to say at legal proceedings or public councils. He cannot contribute to the debate. The wise man, however, has his assigned place at the gate, and his word is heeded. Thus Job, remembering his better days, recalls:

> *When I went out to the* gate *of the city,*
> *when I prepared my seat in the* square,
> *the young men saw me and withdrew,*
> *and the aged rose and stood; . . .*
> *Men listened to me, and waited,*
> *and kept silenee for my* counsel.
> —*Job 29:7–8, 21,* RSV, *emphasis added*

Old men often sat at the gate talking politics, settling legal matters, or just conversing with one another. They were also asked for advice. The situation was similar to that in ancient Rome. Cicero gives us a description when he has Crassus recall how things used to be in the olden days:

> I myself have seen Manius Manilius walking across the *forum;* a signal that he who did so gave all the citizens liberty to ask his advice [*consilium*] upon any subject. To such persons, when thus walking or sitting at home upon their seats of ceremony, all people had free access, not only to consult them upon points of civil law, but even upon the settlement of a daughter in marriage, the purchase of an estate, or the cultivation of a farm, and indeed upon any employment or business whatsoever. Such was the wisdom [*sapientia*] of the well-known elder Publius Crassus, such that of Titus Coruncanius . . . all of whom were supreme pontiffs, so that they were consulted upon all affairs, divine and human.[44]

The similarity here is striking in that the key Latin terms in our text have Hebrew equivalents in Proverbs 1 or Job 29: *forum* corresponds to *rᵉhob* (square), *consilium* is *ᶜeṣah* (advice), and *sapientia* stands for *ḥokmah* (wisdom). Although, according to Job 29, the gate is primarily the place to discuss and decide legal issues—the poor ask the court for legal redress—Job extends his counsel and advice beyond the law when he comforts mourners.[45] Here the humanitarian dimension of helping, comforting, and giving personal advice has been added.

The youths, who had shyly risen and concealed themselves before Job, had probably not left the square at the gate at all. There is always something to be learned by listening carefully to the elders, not just at legal debates, but also at the nightly "palaver."[46] As a matter of course, the young watch all aspects of life in the street and in the public places. Watching people do business is educational and may help a later career. The truly wise person observes life and learns a lesson—"I looked and received instruction"[47]—but does not remain a mere spectator. Student and teacher alike are seen primarily as participants in life. The teacher only once assumes a superior, elevated position, looking out a window down into the street.[48] Does this mean that he gives his warning from inside the house, far removed, so to speak, from the bustle of the street and the unrest of the world? Is he merely a detached observer who notes what happens in the street, commenting on it from a distance? In fact, this is not the case. The window does not compete with street and gate. The window is nothing more than a scenic device. The house and its elevated window turns the teacher into a silent and concealed observer witnessing a lascivious act of temptation that takes place in the open street. Yet the street is the place where wisdom is at home. The teachings of the sages

> did not consist of abstract speculation, were not the result of deep musings about metaphysical relationships, but grew out of the experience of street and market place. Here was the school of practical wisdom, here its home, and here was the place where its truth, endurance and usefulness was tested and demonstrated.[49]

Wisdom, then, is anything but an occult, esoteric theosophy or philosophy. Far from being a secret philosophy, passed on

28

"under the table" to a select few, it is public knowledge that need not shun the marketplace—or the classroom.

Street, gate, and market constitute the arena of public life and are thus places of wisdom. They are places where the careful observer can acquire knowledge. They are places where speakers used to seek an audience. Possibly, they were even places where teachers used to teach.

THE SCHOOL IN THE PUBLIC SQUARE

We know of school buildings and classrooms in Mesopotamia, Ugarit, Egypt, and, of course, Greece. The English *gymnasium* got its name from the Greek athletic school. In southern countries, classes were often held outdoors, at least "when the weather was fine."[50] We are not as well informed about conditions in the ancient Middle East as we are about those in the Greco-Roman world, where students were often taught "publicly in the forum"[51] so that migrant or resident teachers could make themselves seen to be engaged in teaching and readily recruit students for their classes. When the aged Augustine was writing his *Confessions* he could still hear the enticements of the teachers of rhetoric; "Here is where words are learned; here is where eloquence is gained, most essential for persuasion and for the development of opinions."[52] The Roman *forum* and the Greek *agora* were not just places of recruitment, but of instruction as well. Thus the teacher was a familiar sight in the city streets and around the squares, despite the crowds and the noise; for, as an ancient author tells us, "the teachers of letters sit in the streets with their pupils, and nothing prevents the pursuit of teaching and learning, even in so dense a throng."[53] Stores, whose fronts opened toward the columned halls of the forum, frequently served as classrooms. Livy has left a description of this, and Augustine reports that these stores were separated from the noisy street life by only a curtain.[54] Adults were prohibited— even on pain of death in Athens[55]—to enter these easily accessible classrooms during periods of instruction. The teachers did not want to be disturbed in their pedagogic task by constant intrusions from the street.

Figure 3. A thrashing; school scene in the Forum at Pompeii.

A vivid picture of such a school at the forum has been pre-served in an ancient mural, which can be seen in the Naples Museum. In the colonnade that surrounds the forum a small school is in session:

> A boy who has misbehaved, or done his work badly, is shown on the right of the picture hoisted in mid-air by two of his schoolfellows, and is receiving a sound thrashing from a burly adult. The lesson is, like the culprit, temporarily sus-pended, but three other children sit together, on the left of the picture, waiting for it to recommence. They face inwards, with the line of columns behind them, and their reading-books on their knees. Behind these columns, that is, in the open space of the forum, we see four passers-by, two of whom have stopped, not to watch the thrashing, but to see what the children are reading. We are shown the heads and shoulders of these two onlookers; they are peeping round on each side of a column, and are looking down over the chil-dren's shoulders at their papyrus rolls.[56]

30

Martin Nilsson calls the forum "a place as unsuited for instruction as we can think of it, i.e., in the midst of roaring traffic and in the noise of the market." Yet he finds an apology for and indeed a deeper significance in the noisy place. He explains:

> To us, this may seem inappropriate. It is, however, characteristic for the openness of ancient schools toward the pulsing life all around them, and is an ancient legacy. Our schools are hiding behind their four walls and are making a public appearance only at the end of the school year, when annual examinations are held. The Greek school was most vitally and directly related to public life. Thus, it was training its students for future citizenship and introducing them to adult life in which, eventually, they would play their part.[57]

According to Proverbs 1:20f., Wisdom makes her appearance in the streets, in the squares, and at the city gate. The basic reason is that Wisdom must demonstrate her usefulness in the arena of public life. A further reason may have been that the public square and the city gate are places where we find schools, teachers, and classes. In the market square, ancient teachers are known to have taught their students in houses, at market stands, or simply in the open air. Most likely this was no different in Palestine than it was in other Mediterranean countries. In the second century A.D., Rabbi Yehudah the Prince prohibited instruction under the open sky, probably in order to avoid trouble with the Roman occupation forces. The fact that offenders against this prohibition cited Proverbs 1:20, "Wisdom chants in the street,"[58] again indicates that open-air instruction had been customary.

In later Judaism, wisdom was ousted from the marketplace. The Holy Scriptures, the house of teaching, and the synagogue became the privileged places where knowledge might be found, studied, and passed on to the next generation. In Sirach 24:1 personified Wisdom no longer appears in the market square, but in a service of worship. A rabbi of the second century A.D. graphically describes this new setting of wisdom: "If God had given wisdom to the foolish, they would sit in the latrines, the theaters and the public baths talking about it. But God has given Wisdom to the sages who are sitting and talking of it in the synagogues and in the houses of study."[59]

Figure 4. Two teachers supervise a class in a courtyard school of Yemeni Jews in Jerusalem, 1920s.

While this new wisdom, which is actually the knowledge of the Jewish Law, had subjected all aspects of life to its norm, its study was so completely relocated to the academies or schools that it was forbidden even to reflect on the Law when walking in filthy streets.[60] A good scholar would always avoid the hectic atmosphere of urban life and retire to quiet, comfortable places. "My son, do not sit and study at the highest busiest point of the town" was the first of a series of advices Rabbi Akiba gave his son, who was to become a scholar himself. The practical-minded Akiba knew his colleagues and thus also advised his son never to live in a town whose leaders are scholars.[61] The wisdom of scholars is respected, but one does not readily rely on them in practical matters.

32

Thus what had been practical knowledge for coping with life became "book knowledge" for coping with texts and the almost impenetrable jungle of religious law and its interpretation. Life orientation had given way to text orientation. Wisdom was now something concerning books and scholarship. It was the domain of sages who retired to the stillness of their study, while "out there in constant delusion, roars the busy world" (Eichendorff).

CHAPTER 4

The Rhetoric of Teaching

"The untutored kill themselves by their disobedience, the stubbornness of fools destroys them [Prov. 1:32]." This sentence is an aphorism of the kind collected in Proverbs 10—30, which does in fact include similar sayings.[1] We know that the schools were fond of using wisdom adages and that the teachers put together extensive collections. Not only the form of the saying, which is arranged as a couplet, but also the subject matter may best be understood in the context of school and classroom instruction. The aphorism takes us to the classroom and has one participate in the interaction of teacher and student. The verse quoted may be seen as the words of an instructor struggling with disobedient and stubborn students. Pointing out the consequences of their actions, the teacher tries to get them to change their attitude and behavior. Of course, this is the objective of the whole poem as well.

The classroom setting can be established for other parts of Wisdom's address. "Because I speak, and you refuse [to listen], I lift my hand [in warning], and no one heeds [vs. 24]" is a clear case in point. The language here is that of an infuriated teacher, and verses 25 and 29–30 contain the same angry note. The students are obstinate and uninterested in learning. Their teacher is understandably disappointed and upset. Wisdom's voice is that of the schoolmaster.

It is not surprising to find anger, threats, and reprimands

34

being expressed in the classroom. As we know from ancient Egyptian sources, they are among the most ancient tools of education—just like the thrashing to which teachers sometimes resorted.[2] None of these measures should be taken to imply resignation on the part of the teacher; rather, the teachers understood them as tools of correction and education that would eventually bring the student on the right path.

The language used in the classroom is specialized. Whether we are considering the classroom, the temple, the royal court, or the market square—in all these places we find a specialized form of language in use, with its own typical vocabulary and expressions. Speaking to students in the classroom the teacher needs other linguistic tools than the scribe who composes letters, for instance, or the prophet who utters oracles. Every area of life makes its own demands of language and develops its own linguistic tradition. Yet these specialized languages rarely remain isolated from one another. They are permeable one to the other and in constant flux within the general language. "You hate discipline, and you cast my words behind you" may well have its original setting in the classroom and in the teacher's mouth; in Psalm 50:17, RSV, it is quoted as said by God. Prophetic literature especially is filled with echoes of what I propose to call the language of school and instruction. Here are some examples of reproach and reprimand:

> *She [Jerusalem] listens to no voice,*
> *she accepts no correction.*
>
> *—Zephaniah 3:2,* RSV

> *Though I [teach] them persistently they [do] not [listen]*
> *to receive instruction.*
>
> *—Jeremiah 32:33,* RSV

> *They [do] not listen or incline their ear, but [stiffen]*
> *their neck, that they might not hear and receive*
> *instruction.*
>
> *—Jeremiah 17:23,* RSV

The prophet or the prophet's god often acts as a teacher and therefore uses the language of instruction. It would be a mistake and a serious misunderstanding to reverse this relationship and make Wisdom and the ancient Israelite schoolmasters dependent on the language of prophecy. Traces of the language of school and instruction are almost ever present in the Bible.

THE TEACHER'S ASSERTION OF AUTHORITY

"He who listens to me will dwell secure and will be spared panic and terror [Prov. 1:33]." These are the words of a teacher who is sure of his instruction and wants to stimulate students to learn. "My son, do not forget my teaching," the instructor says elsewhere; "for length of days and years of [successful] life and abundant welfare will they give you."[3]

Teachers speaking in this fashion are quite sure of themselves. They are confident that what they have to say is important to their students and will vitally affect their students' lives. Those who are familiar with the psychology of advertising may become skeptical and object that teachers are merely trying to persuade their students by any means at their disposal. There is some truth in this objection. Teachers try to persuade, if not convince, their students. Yet the teachers' claim to communicate what is essential and vitally important to their students should not be dismissed as mere pedagogic trickery. There is more to it. Both in Israel and ancient Egypt[4] the role of the teacher involved more than the transmission of basic skills, such as reading, writing, and arithmetic. Had this been the sole task of a teacher, his standing in society would have been as low as that of an elementary instructor in classical Greece and Rome. In Egypt and Israel, teachers were responsible for the moral instruction, guidance, and character formation of their students. Like the teacher-cum-priests of the medieval monastic schools of Europe, they functioned as "spiritual fathers." As such, the teacher was superior in more than a mere patriarchal sense; he enjoyed what Latin writers call *auctoritas* (i.e., he was in a recognized position of authority).[5] Because of his greater insight and keener sense of responsibility, the teacher lay claim to the inner life of the student. Egyptian teachers, as we know them from ancient Egyptian instruction literature, and the schoolmasters of Israel were

36

neither mere drillmasters of basic skills nor sophisticated tutors of questionable rhetorical techniques and polite manners, but communicators of *wisdom*. Wisdom is more than cleverness and career-oriented knowledge. "Wise counsel," explains a philosopher, "is necessarily given with a sense of a deep moral responsibility."[6]

The wisdom communicated by teachers does not originate in them nor is it a product of their brilliance. It is the tradition, and nothing else, that is being passed from teacher to student. The teacher's individuality, therefore, does not really matter, even though the teacher speaks emphatically in the first person. The voice of the teacher is the voice of tradition and thus, in a sense, beyond individuality. The ancient Near Eastern world, Egypt in particular, is not interested in individuality, peculiarity of character, or the "confessions" kind of biographical reflection known from Augustine and Rousseau. All this is preempted by the general, the objectively valid, and the universally true. Thus in the visual arts of Egypt we fail to find lifelike portraits of individuals. *Auctoritas,* therefore, implies the renunciation of individuality and, more important, the ability to exercise power over others. The reason is that *auctoritas* is based only on the validity of the tradition, not on the brilliance and ingenuity of the teacher or some other external influence. Tradition here does not simply mean that which has been uncritically accepted from an immediately preceding generation. As was observed by T. S. Eliot, tradition "cannot be inherited, and if you want it you must obtain it by great labour."[7] An individual teacher bears witness to the tradition after he or she has thoroughly studied it and experienced its value and validity in life.This is the only reason the names of the authors—like Ptahhotep, Khety, or Any—have been attached to Egyptian teaching manuals. Ptahhotep is the witness, not the author, in a modern sense. Outside Egypt, the ancient Near Eastern literature generally is anonymous, for the culture that produced it did not develop the concept of literary authorship or of a copyright that could be violated by plagiarism.

Tradition and *auctoritas* influence and indeed structure the relationship between teacher and student as well as the teaching method. Students submit not so much to the authority of an older person, but to the dignity of the subject matter communicated by the teacher. When it comes to the content of what is taught, students and teachers find themselves on an equal level. Admonishing the student and appealing to him in rational discourse, the teacher places himself on an equal level with his student. The assertion that "he who listens to me will dwell secure [Prov. 1:33]" does not imply that the teacher is an all-powerful individual, but sees him as one who communicates tradition. Because the teacher appeals without forcing acceptance of his teaching, the student is free to take on himself the guilt of ignoring it.

As a preserver of tradition, the teacher occupies a respected position in society. At King Ahab's court the tutors of princes are mentioned along with the rulers and elders of the capital city, Samaria, and the teachers of King David's sons are listed by name in a roster of high-ranking Judean court officials.[8] Even the most humble instructor of Talmudic times lays claim to this image, although at times a distinction between theoretical esteem and practical disdain of teachers may be noted.[9]

"He who listens to me will dwell secure and will be spared panic and terror [Prov. 1:33]." These self-confident words make sense only in the light of the teacher's authority and superior wisdom. They reflect his position as mediator of tradition and witness to its validity. Even the "I" form used by the teacher in a way transcends individuality. Coming from Wisdom, Proverbs 1:33 has the sound of majesty, thus giving the words even greater weight than they would have had being spoken by an ordinary teacher. The authority of various teachers and counselors may have led to conflict situations.[10] There is no possibility of conflict when Wisdom herself speaks. Her words carry final, irrefutable authority. Even though Wisdom continues to argue, appeal, and justify, she does not actually place herself on the same level as her students. Thus the words of a teacher spoken by Wisdom are given a new emphasis. Coming from a teacher, the sentence "they would have none of my advice, and reject all of my teaching [vs. 30]" does not sound unusual at all. Yet, coming from Wisdom, these words are barely distinguishable from the reproach made by God in a prophetic oracle: "They refuse to know me [Jer. 9:6, RSV]."

38

The affinity between the word of Wisdom and the word of Yahweh is evident in Proverbs 1:28:

> *Then they will call upon me, but I will not answer;*
> *they will seek me, but will not find me.*

The students call on the teacher only after they are in trouble. They go to his house,[11] but they do not find him, for the teacher does not want to have anything to do with those who have refused him. The words in the teacher's speech are quite similar to those in passages speaking of Yahweh:

> *With their flocks and herds they shall go to seek [Yahweh],*
> *but they will not find him.[12]*
>
> —*Hosea 5:6,* RSV
>
> *Though they cry in my ears with a loud voice, I will not*
> *hear them.[13]*
>
> —*Ezekiel 8:18,* RSV

Just as men and women call on and seek to find God in times of trouble, so the desperate student seeks his teacher—or Wisdom. In monotheistic Judaism it would have been either blasphemous or meaningless to call on Wisdom in the same sense as one would call on God in prayer. Yet in polytheistic circles of preexilic Israel, Wisdom must have been regarded as a goddess. This line of argument is pursued further in the final section of this book.

ELEMENTS OF HEBREW RHETORIC

As a public speaker, Wisdom uses the stylistic devices common in Hebrew rhetoric. Especially the opening and closing sections of her speech follow a pattern found elsewhere in biblical and ancient oratory. Another noteworthy stylistic feature is the change from direct address to impersonal comment. The speech begins as follows:

> *How long, immature ones, will you love immaturity?*
> *[Will] mischief-makers delight in mischief-making*
> *And fools hate knowledge?*
>
> —*Proverbs 1:22*

It is easy to imagine that a teacher has to ask his noisy crowd of students to pay attention at the beginning of class. A speaker at a public assembly has a similar problem.[14] There is none of this here. Wisdom presents the sort of noble bearing that instantly commands attention; reminiscent of Job, at whose appearance in public "the princes refrained from talking, and laid their hand on their mouth; the voice of the nobles was hushed, and their tongue cleaved to the roof of their mouth [Job 29:9–10, RSV]." There is no lengthy salutation either. Wisdom begins her speech with a direct, rhetorically effective question: "How long . . .?" She calls the listener to account and gives no chance for rebuttal, an opening that has the effect of immediately asserting the speaker's authority over the audience. The aggressive and provocative question, "How long will you . . .?" was known to speakers as an elegant opening in Rome[15] as well as in Israel. It is the opening of Cicero's speech *Against Catilina,* of Moses' speech before the king of Egypt, and of the prophet Elijah's harangue to an Israelite crowd gathered on Mount Carmel. Joshua uses it, and three speeches in the book of Job are introduced in this fashion.[16] In one instance the rhetorical question serves to enhance the contrast between the angry teacher and the sleeping sluggard: "How long will you lie there, O sluggard? When will you arise from your sleep [Prov. 6:9, RSV]?" Elsewhere a teacher asks, "How long will you be deprived of wisdom's food, how long will you endure such bitter thirst?"[17]

Every speaker knows that the opening words of a speech must be planned with the utmost care. A teacher may well have asked his students in class, "How long, immature ones, will you love immaturity?" in order to motivate learning. That is the purpose of the sentence in the poem. Spoken by Wisdom, it has a much more compelling and noble ring than the words of a mere schoolmaster.

The conclusion of the speech (Proverbs 1:32–33), like the introduction, has been composed for rhetorical effect:

> *For the immature kill themselves by their disobedience,*
> *The stubbornness of fools destroys them—*
> *But he who listens to me will dwell secure*
> *And will be spared panic and terror.*

40

Conclusions of this kind are common in Hebrew rhetoric. The term summary appraisal[18] has been coined for them, since the conclusion summarizes and assesses what has been said. As in the case of the Wisdom speech, summary appraisals begin with "for," offering a final justification of the argument developed earlier. An example similar to the text just cited is the conclusion of a didactic poem in Proverbs 5:21–23, RSV:

> *For a man's ways are before the eyes of [Yahweh],*
> *and he watches all his paths.*
> *The iniquities of the wicked ensnare him,*
> *and he is caught in the toils of his sin.*
> *He dies for lack of discipline,*
> *and because of his great folly he is lost.*

This technique is well known in the poetry of classical antiquity. Two examples of summary appraisals from Sophocles may suffice to illustrate: "The gods love goodness, and abhor all that is evil," and "Wicked payments work their own revenge."[19] These maxims are "final lessons" designed to reinforce and underline the preceding argument. Far from being merely decorative, they function as final persuaders. The saying supports and emphasizes what has been said, giving weight to what seems self-evident. Proverbs 1:32f., however, differ from other, merely negative appraisals in that they include a positive element: "He who listens to me will dwell secure and will be spared panic and terror." This form of commending generally is used only as an introduction.[20]

Another rhetorical peculiarity of the Wisdom speech is the transition from "talking to" the audience in the second person (vss. 22–27) to "talking about" them in the third person (vss. 22b, 28–33). Wisdom wavers between proximity and distance. This kind of inconsistency is often found as a consciously used stylistic device in Canaanite texts. The use of the third person serves as a form of "indirect address" that establishes or respects a certain distance between speaker and listener. It is easy to understand why a petitioner before the king would speak in the third person, saying, "The king, my lord, appointed me," instead of "You have appointed me," or why a speaker would talk about his audience rather than addressing his hearers directly.[21] In the same vein, Wisdom speaks about her audience. It is no doubt a mark of rhetorical skill that she does not bluntly address her listeners as ne'er-do-wells and fools (vs. 22), but talks about them as if she meant someone else. This is also true for the change of person after verse 27. Those who are incorrigible are mentioned only for the sake of the wise. The fate of the ne'er-do-wells serves as a lesson for others. One can also note that the passage in the second person (vss. 22–27) is balanced by a passage of equal length in the third person (vss. 28–33). After Wisdom has proclaimed calamity she uses only the third person in reporting the result. She thereby reestablishes her distance from the people addressed and keeps this distance.[22]

CHAPTER 5

Brief Commentary on Proverbs 1:20–33

The first four lines of the poem announce that Wisdom is speaking:

> 20 *[Lady] Wisdom¹ chants on the street,*
> *In the square she raises her voice,*
> 21 *At the top of the busy street (?) she cries out,*
> *At the entrance of the city gate she speaks.*

The opening verses of the poems in Proverbs 8 and 9 are similar. In all three poems Wisdom makes her appearance publicly and in the city. The kind of wisdom presented to the reader in the didactic discourses of Proverbs 1—7 also has an urban setting. The place where wisdom may be acquired and where it must prove itself is the city. Wisdom, then, is basically the sagacity and skill needed by anyone who wants to cope with life in a public, urban setting. The poem does not tell us where exactly Wisdom is going to appear. Street, square, and city gates are mentioned, and perhaps, depending on the correctness of our translation, busy street life.² Wherever there is sufficient space under the open skies, where the people living in the city are likely to gather, there Wisdom may make her appeal. We should, of course, think of the cities of ancient Israel as anything but spacious. At the time of the monarchy, Jerusalem certainly did not have a Hyde Park with its speaker's corner, where anyone could stand up to address the public, provided the topic attracted an audience. Jerusalem was much too cramped for this, and the other cities were certainly no larger. Most likely the city had only one open square—the one just inside or outside the city gate. Here a speaker could stand in the middle of a crowd—or perhaps stand on the city wall and address the crowd gathered below. As a rule, public life took place around the city gate. The merchants could find space to display their goods there, people could meet to talk or to attend a court session; and orators might also be looking for an audience there. School may even have been held there, either in market stalls or under the open sky.

Among the various expressions used to introduce Wisdom's speech, there are two that seem to give the passage its own particular coloring. In the first place it is said that Wisdom, like a public speaker, seeks to draw public attention to something by raising her voice.[3] Second, we are told that Wisdom *chants*. The root meaning of the Hebrew verb *ranan* is "to recite or chant a poem or prayer."[4] The Septuagint, therefore, makes Wisdom "sing" (*humneitai* in Proverbs 1:20; 8:3). This translation is quite correct. Wisdom does not speak in prose, but recites poetry. Her speech is in stylized, poetic form, and poems are either recited or chanted. The use of *ranan* may also hint at the teacher's method of instruction: he made the class recite or chant the didactic texts in unison.[5]

It takes a master poet to suggest in these few words that the public places of the city are the proper setting for learning, that here learning must also demonstrate its worth, and that Wisdom is about to speak or chant in poetic form.

Unlike some of the prophets, however, Wisdom does not entice her audience "like one who sings love songs with a beautiful voice and plays well on an instrument [Ezek. 33:32, RSV]." Instead, she surprises them with an aggressive rhetorical question:

22   *"How long, immature ones, will you love immaturity?*
     [Will] mischief-makers delight in mischief-making[6]
     And fools hate knowledge?"

Wisdom uses the language of the classroom. Like a teacher, she talks to young men who have yet to trade their immaturity for the wisdom that both school and life can provide. The teacher knows that these young men are quite content in their immaturity. They have no desire to strive for higher things or to attain wisdom. Like fools, they are wedded to their immaturity; they are even enamored by it. Naming the "immature" young man along with the mischief-maker and the fool is to say that being simple or immature is not far from being bad and stupid. If a young man insists on remaining a simpleton, he will soon be numbered among the incorrigible good-for-nothings and the ne'er-do-wells. (Note that the persons addressed—the real or potential mischief-makers—are young *men*. Nothing is said about young women, who are never referred to in the book of Proverbs, except as seducers and adulteresses. One exception is the poetic praise of the perfect and dutiful woman in Proverbs 31, a text that clearly betrays its male perspective.)

The rhetorical question, as is usual in oratory, is followed by a request to listen and an introductory announcement of the speech:

> 23 *Give heed to my admonition!*
> *Yes, I will speak my mind to you,*
> *I will make known my lesson to you.*[7]

This announcement is followed by an angry harangue. The speaker's anger and displeasure are already apparent in the introduction: the Hebrew terms for "admonition" and "mind" can take on the connotation of "reproof" and "anger." Yet the displeasure of the speaker only becomes explicit in the passage that follows:

> 24 *Because I speak, and you refuse [to listen],*[8]
> *I lift my hand [in warning], and no one heeds,*
> 25 *And you would have none of my advice,*
> *Ignoring all my teaching,*
> 26 *Therefore I will laugh out loud*[9] *at your calamity,*
> *I will mock, when panic strikes you,*

²⁷ *When panic strikes you like a whirlwind,*
When distress and anguish come upon you.

Here we have the words of an angry teacher. She is fed up with unwilling, inattentive students and is venting her anger. Four phrases are used to describe the basically negative attitude of the students: they refuse to listen, no one heeds, they would have none of their teacher's advice, they ignore all her teaching. This is not an uncommon attitude for students. Punctuating her words by raising her hands in a threatening gesture,[10] the teacher attempts to correct her students—but to no avail.

There is a necessary balance of give and take which implies that the wicked must suffer the consequences of their deeds. Although it may not seem so at the time, misfortune has a way of appearing out of nowhere, like a sudden storm that may cause a dangerous flash flood in a Palestinian wadi.[11] At any rate, in Wisdom's world of order and design, random events cannot help but appear to be utterly dreadful.[12] There is nothing the teacher can do to prevent the misfortune of her students. Wisdom does not even try. Once calamity is upon him, an evildoer will be laughed at and ridiculed, for one man's loss is another's gain. In this case, laughter is a serious matter because it expresses a moral judgment. Here, laughter rejoices in the fact that the wicked are getting their just deserts. Those who laugh rejoice in the moral order of the universe. Job 22:16, 19, RSV, expresses this view in a particularly striking way:

> *They were snatched away before their time . . .*
> *The righteous see it and are glad,*
> *the innocent laugh them to scorn.*[13]

The cause of laughter need not be as drastic an event as the end of an evil person. The misfortune of the wicked becomes an occasion for scorn and laughter. For instance, one may mockingly laugh at those who are unable to complete the simple work of building a tower because they have failed to work out the correct cost.[14] To distinguish this kind of laughter from the merely humorous variety, the label "elenctic" (i.e., correcting and persuading) has been proposed.[15] Philosopher Henri

Bergson notes that laughing, in this sense, has the connotation of punishment rather than that of rejoicing in something good. "Laughter," he explains, "is, above all, a corrective. Being intended to humiliate, it must make a painful impression on the person against whom it is directed. By laughter, society avenges itself for the liberties taken with it. It would fail in its object if it bore the stamp of sympathy and kindness."[16]

In one instance, ridicule with the intent of exposing another person was given legal status. The levirate law provides that if a man refuses to marry his brother's widow, she shall "pull his sandal off his foot, and spit in his face . . . [and] his house shall be called in Israel, The house of him that had his sandal pulled off."[17] Thus the law makes a public laughingstock of that man. Wisdom's laughter seems best described in terms of this kind of corrective and punitive ridicule.

In the last part of Wisdom's speech the untutored young men are no longer addressed directly, but are referred to in the third person. The speaker moves from proximity to distance. We may infer that those who had been addressed, or at least some of them, have turned against the speaker and are no longer listening. Yet Wisdom does not go on talking to herself like a speaker whose audience has melted away. Instead, she expounds to anyone who is willing to listen the misfortune that will happen to those who have turned their backs on her.

Here again, Wisdom uses the language of instruction. She starts with a reference to the students' response when they are in trouble. It is then that they will remember their teachers and seek their help. Suddenly, the once-unwilling student admits that "I did not listen to the voice of my teachers [Prov. 5:13, RSV]." But the teacher no longer grants her assistance. It is too late:

> 28 *Then they will call upon me, but I will not answer;*
> *They will seek me, but will not find me.*

The teacher is as proud as the Assyrian king Esarhaddon. After repeated warnings the seventh-century B.C. king was victorious in a campaign against a rebellious prince and then refused to accept the loser's submission. It was too late. An inscription records the king's words: "I did not listen to his pleading, his supplication I did not accept, and his requests I did not grant." Speaking to the rebel, the king asks, "Did ever you hear a mighty king speak his word twice? Now I, a king more than mighty, have written you thrice; yet you have not heeded the words of my mouth."[18] Yahweh's pride is also like that of the monarch. He will no longer hear the supplications of those who despise his word as proclaimed by his prophets. In the end, Yahweh no longer sends prophets to warn and admonish his people, but executes punishment.[19] There is, then, a common pattern to what teachers, kings and gods do. The teacher goes on to justify her decision:

> 29 *Since they hate knowledge*
> *And do not love the fear of Yahweh [originally: fear of the gods?],*
> 30 *Would have none of my advice,*
> *And reject all of my teaching,*
> 31 *Therefore they shall eat the fruit of their [wicked] way,*
> *And be sated with [the fruit of] their own devices.*
> 32 *For the immature kill themselves by their disobedience,*
> *The stubbornness of fools destroys them—*
> 33 *But he who listens to me will dwell secure*
> *And will be spared panic and terror.*

The substance of these lines is that those who pay heed to Wisdom will not suffer misfortune, and those who refuse to listen will suffer the consequences. The poet does not put it that bluntly. Wisdom uses a number of impressive images, heightening the effect by repeating the same thought in different ways. There are four versions of the complaint "they reject my instruction": they hate knowledge, do not love the fear of Yahweh, would have none of my advice, reject all of my teaching. "Fear of Yahweh" seems to replace an original "fear of the gods,"[20] both expressions referring to the teacher's instruction; perhaps the teacher also intends to add religious disrepute to the problems of Wisdom's unwilling students. The idea that "they will suffer the consequences" is also stated four times: they shall eat the fruit of their way (that is, they have made their bed and now must lie on it), they will be sated with their own devices, they commit suicide by their disobedience, their stubbornness destroys them. For an Israelite, the metaphors of "fruit" and "eating" clearly and graphically express the notion of responsibility for one's own fortune or misfortune. "A perverse man will be filled with the fruit of his ways," as Proverbs 14:14, RSV, has it.[21] A particularly drastic expression of the same idea implies suicide in verse 32: his disobedience becomes the fool's own deadly enemy, killing the untutored in the end. A similar expression, "gain by violence takes away the life of its possessors,"[22] shows that the poet is fond of such pointed sayings. They provide an effective contrast for the closing sentence, which promises a life secure and free of dread to the student who listens (i.e., pays heed and obeys).

The objective of the speech as a whole is to induce students to accept the lesson that is taught. By means of the poetic form and his appeal to Wisdom as the ultimate authority, the teacher draws the necessary attention to himself and to his subject matter. Even though the student may miss the finer points of rhetoric and style, he cannot ignore the threatening hand of the teacher (vs. 24). Wisdom—as the teacher presents her and has her speak—does not have the exact characteristics of an ordinary human figure. She comes closest to a teacher who instructs students in the city square and who, on occasion, tries to correct their conduct with a thorough tongue-lashing. Yet the image of that kind of teacher compares quite poorly with Wisdom. To be sure, the language of classroom and instruction permeates the speech. There is no way of overlooking this. However, the figure talking in the poem is not just an ordinary teacher, but Wisdom in person, whose voice carries greater dignity and higher authority. Wisdom does not shout like an angry and frustrated teacher; she "chants" (vs. 20).

When one compares the didactive discourses of Proverbs 1—7 with Wisdom's own voice, another unique feature of her speech becomes clear. While Wisdom corrects and invites her students, the teacher of the didactic discourses lays out specific rules of human conduct as part of his lesson.[23] The initial invitation and concluding maxim[24] have their equivalents in Wisdom's speech, but in the latter, specific instruction is replaced by the more general theme of relating acts and consequences. Unlike the didactic discourses, Wisdom does not seek to teach rules. She speaks only in order to motivate students to listen and learn. There is no other aim. The purpose of her rhetoric is winning over, even propagandizing, her audience. In all this, Wisdom does not advocate a particular profession—like that of a scribe or civil servant[25]—or recommend a particular professional ethic; instead, she pleads for a wisdom that is universally valid and binding. It follows that whoever rejects her teaching is not only a poor student and a failure, unfit for public office, but also an evil human being. The contrast drawn between those who listen to wisdom and those who are good-for-nothings shows a total contradiction. There is no middle ground between the two extremes.

Wisdom seeks a larger audience than she is able to find in the school. She appears at the city square, where she expects to find both students, who may be formed into a class for instruction, and other people, for whom—above and beyond school—the lessons of wisdom are still relevant. Even someone who has never been formally instructed in wisdom should know and understand its requirements. Wisdom indicates the essence of her teaching with a few, almost synonymous terms such as knowledge, fear of the gods, advice, and teaching (vss. 29f.). Apparently, a few key terms suffice to indicate a well-known subject matter. Everyone who has things to do at the city gate knows only too well what Wisdom is talking about and why she pleads her cause. Wisdom, the ability to cope, is germane to life.

PART TWO
WISDOM AS A GODDESS

(Proverbs 8)

The Poem Proverbs 8:1–36

1   *It is [Lady] Wisdom calling*
    [Lady] Understanding raising her voice.
2   *On the walls [of the city], on the paths,*
    In the streets she takes her stand.
3   *Beside the gates, at the entrance of the city,*
    At the portals she chants:
4   *"To you, O men, I appeal,*
    My speech is for [all] the sons of men!
5   *O immature ones, learn shrewdness,*
    O foolish ones, instruct [your] minds!
6   *Listen! I speak [teach] noble things,*
    And from my lips comes what is right.
7   *What my mouth utters is reliable,*
    Wickedness is abhorrent to my lips.
8   *All the words of my mouth are just,*
    None of them perverse or crooked;
9   *All are straight[forward] to him who is intelligent*
    And right to those who have attained knowledge.
10 *Prefer my instruction to silver*
    And knowledge to the finest gold!
11 *For wisdom is better than [red] coral,*
    No jewels can compare with her.
12 *I am [Lady] Wisdom. I am shrewd,*
    I have attained much skill.

13   To fear Yahweh is to hate evil.
Pride, arrogance, and the evil way
And perverted speech: [these] I hate.

14   *I know how to plan and to execute plans,*
I have insight, I am mighty.

15   *Through me kings reign*
And rulers issue just decrees.

16   *Through me officials do their work,*
Noble men and all who are responsible for order.

17   *Those who love me[1] I love*
And those who seek me will find me.

18   *Immeasurable riches are with me,*
Choice treasures and prosperity.

19   *My fruit is better than fine gold,*
My produce better than choice silver.

20   *I walk on the way of order,*
Along the paths of justice,

21   *Endowing with wealth those who love me,*
Filling their treasuries.

22   *Yahweh [originally, El?] begot me when he began to be*
active [literally, at the beginning of his way],
In the earliest days of his creation, long ago.

23   *Ages ago* he fashioned me[2] *[in the womb],*
At the beginning, at the origin of earth.

24   *There was still no sea*
Full of water when I was born.

25   *Before the [foundations of] the mountains were sunk,*
Before the hills I was born,

26   *When he had not yet made earth and fields,*
Or the world's first clump of clay.

27   *When he set the heavens into place I was there,*
When he drew a circle on the face of the sea;

28   *When he made firm the clouds above,*
And fixed[3] *the fountains and the sea [below];*

29   *When he assigned the sea its limits*
So that the waters never transgress his command;
When he marked out the foundations of the earth—

30   *Then I was at his side as an infant,*

> [His] delight day by day,
> Frolicking before him at all times,
31   Frolicking on his earth,
> Delighting in the sons of men.
32   Now, sons, listen to me!
> Happy are they who keep my ways!
33   Listen to [my] instruction and become wise!
> Do not spurn [it]!
34   Happy is the man who listens to me,
> Standing at my door day by day,
> Waiting [for me] at my threshold!
35   For he who acquires me attains[4] life
> And obtains favor from Yahweh [originally, the gods?].
36   But he who misses me, hurts himself;
> All who hate me love death [originally, love Mot]."

Proverbs 8 is closely related to the poems in Proverbs 1 and 9 in that they are all about Wisdom. She addresses men, and her voice may be heard in the street and especially around the city gate. Yet there are significant differences. Proverbs 8 is longer than the other two poems taken together. Wisdom's proud self-portrayal in Proverbs 8 is unique and unparalleled. While our first poem, in Proverbs 1, hardly looks beyond school and classroom, we are now in the world of rank and influence, of politics and government. Even the king is mentioned as someone who depends on Wisdom and her favors. But not even this is sufficient for Wisdom. She does not hide her infinite superiority over the human race: she has been present at the creation of the world. In this poem, then, Wisdom takes on a much greater role than that of a teacher. While remaining on one level a teacher, she is also a goddess who judges the rulers and dwells in the presence of the creator god. As the poem proceeds, more and more solemn statements are piled up and an intense poetic feeling is created. There is a move from classroom and city square to the world of government and another move from government to the mythology of creation. Let me begin by disentangling some of Wisdom's multiple roles by looking at her rhetoric.

Two Kinds of Rhetoric: Didactic and Divine

Like the poem in Proverbs 1, the poem in Proverbs 8 begins with the announcement of a speech to be given by Wisdom. In both texts Wisdom appears in the streets and at the city gate. Again, in both texts she uses didactic language. In Proverbs 8:4–11 we can clearly hear the teacher's voice asking for attention and recruiting students from the street.

Verse 11—"Wisdom is better than red coral"—may be called a competitive aphorism. One may imagine, perhaps, that the teacher who uses it as a slogan for his profession is standing next to the sellers of all sorts of goods, and that the lesson he is trying to sell is in fact competing with other items offered for sale. "Prefer my instruction to silver!" may mean, for instance, that the teacher is hawking his lessons next to a booth selling precious jewelry. This kind of competitive aphorism makes sense only in a situation in which jewelry and silverware are an expensive but affordable luxury for the propertied urban elite. Wisdom, the schoolmasters assert, can stand comparison with even the most precious and expensive of items. Competitive aphorisms of the same kind are common. "To get [to buy] wisdom is better than [to get, buy] gold; to get [buy] understanding is to be chosen rather than silver," says one saying, and another one asserts that "the gain from it [wisdom] is better than gain from silver." And again, "she [wisdom] is more precious than jewels, and nothing

56

you can desire compares with her."[1] We do not have to go as far as putting wisdom *above* gold. Wisdom can be given equal billing with the most precious jewelry. Thus instruction is like "a fair garland for your head, and pendants for your neck [Prov. 1:9, RSV]." Given the competitive situation of the marketplace, however, the formula "prefer A to B" is likely to be more to the point, particularly since the student's attention has to be drawn not only to the (priceless) treasures of the mind, but also to the teacher's instruction, which, naturally, implies paying tuition.[2]

The teacher's introductory speech ends with verse 11. Wisdom does not use didactic language again until verses 32–36, in the conclusion of the poem. Expressions like "Happy are they . . ." and the form of address "sons" are typical for this kind of language. The phrase "Now, sons, listen to me" in addition to the hint as to deadly consequences for refusing to listen are found both here and in the concluding section of another teacher's discourse in Proverbs.[3]

The rest of the poem, which is sandwiched between the school rhetoric in verses 1–11 and 32–36, is made up of a different kind of language. Wisdom is no longer presented as a teacher, but as a goddess who introduces herself as a patroness of high-ranking state officials and kings. She also refers to her divine pedigree, using the language of myth. The proud self-presentation of a divine being is not unknown elsewhere in the Old Testament. "I am the God of your father, the God of Abraham," says Yahweh, revealing himself to Moses; "I am [Yahweh] your God, who brought you out of the land of Egypt, out of the house of bondage [Exod. 3:6; 20:2, RSV]" is the familiar opening of the decalogue. In a polytheistic world a deity appearing in a vision or a dream, or in the dreamlike reality of a mythic tale, has to identify herself or himself. Such self-presentations can take on grand dimensions in what scholars have termed the "self-praise of a god," a genre well known from Mesopotamian sources. Especially in Second Isaiah we hear the echo of this boastful genre. The prophet delights in having his god present himself: "I am [Yahweh], who made all things, who stretched out the heavens alone, who spread out the earth—Who was with me [Isa. 44:24, RSV]?"[4]

Yahweh is not alone in his use of the proud first-person style.

"I am a son of the wise [Isa. 19:11, rsv]," a high-ranking official says to the king of Egypt. Ezekiel has the king of Tyre say, "I am a god, I sit in the seat of the gods, in the heart of the seas [Ezek. 28:2, rsv]." Elsewhere, the same prophet presents Tyre, the city personified, as saying of itself, "I am perfect in beauty [Ezek. 27:3, rsv]." There are numerous parallel passages in literature from Mesopotamia, Egypt, Palestine, and Syria. While scholarship has failed to produce an exact model for Wisdom's speech,[5] there are several Mesopotamian texts in which kings use a similar rhetoric that is everything else but modest. Around 2000 b.c. the Sumerian king of the city of Ur in hymnic self-praise wrote:

> *I, Shulgi, am the life[giver] of Sumer,*
> *A king, who far and wide brooks no rival,*
> *Nay, I can add, whatever is from me, that is great!*
> *To me, king, what can there happen to disturb me?*
> *I have intelligence and energy in extraordinary measure*
> *for the right guidance [of the people].[6]*

The eighth-century b.c. Assyrian king Sargon almost rivals his Sumerian colleague:

> I, Sargon, king of the four regions [of the world], ruler [literally, shepherd] of Assyria, . . . the rightful king, whose words are gracious, whose aversion [abomination] is falsehood, from whose mouth words bringing evil and harm do not emanate; most wise prince of the regions [of the earth], who was created in wisdom and understanding.[7]

Another text is equally boastful; again it is Sargon who speaks:

> I am powerful, I am all-powerful, I am a hero, I am gigantic, I am colossal, I am honored, I am magnified, I am without an equal among all kings, the chosen one of gods Assur, Nabu and Marduk, called of Sin, favorite of Anu.[8]

It is in this sultry atmosphere of bombastic divine and royal self-praise that we have to understand Wisdom's rhetoric in verses 12–21. The wisdom injunction, "Let another praise you, and not your own mouth [Prov. 27:2, rsv]," is not relevant for kings, gods, and goddesses. Far from copying a foreign model and

58

adapting it to suit Wisdom, the poet uses a common literary style that flourished in a world in which nobody prevented kings and gods from boasting of superior wisdom and unrivaled power, saying, "I am powerful, I am all-powerful, I am a hero," or "I have insight, I am mighty, through me kings reign and rulers issue just decrees."

CHAPTER 8

Wisdom: Patroness of Kings and Witness of Creation

What kind of goddess is Wisdom to proclaim her divine nature with such boastful rhetoric? Two of her assertions provide the clue: "By me kings reign" and "I love those who love me." Wisdom is the divine patroness of rulers to whom she grants sovereignty and with whom she entertains a relationship of mutual trust and love. The Assyrian king Assurbanipal II, for instance, attributed his position of sovereignty to the favor granted by goddess Ishtar. "I was born amid mountains which no one knew," he says, referring to his nonroyal descent. He then continues:

> But then, O Ishtar, fearsome mistress of the gods,
> Thou didst single me out with the glance of thine eyes;
> Thou didst desire to see me rule.
> Thou didst take me from among the mountains.
> Thou didst call me to be a shepherd king of men.
> Thou didst grant me the scepter of justice.[1]

Elsewhere, Ishtar is called "she who gives scepter, throne and royal power [?] to every king."[2] In Egypt the concept of the king's divine patroness was also quite common. Hathor, Isis, and Neith are frequently mentioned as having this function, but any other goddess could serve equally well, including Maat. The goddess Maat, who stands for cosmic order and social harmony,

60

justice, and truth, is a particularly apt symbol of rule and state as understood by the Egyptians.

Ancient texts emphasize the loving relationship between king and goddess, asserting, for instance, that a king is "beloved of Hathor, Mistress of Denderah," or that "the one whom her [Isis'] heart loves, has been chosen to occupy the throne."[3] In iconography the king of Egypt is often shown with a goddess embracing him from behind or shielding him with two large wings. Similar scenes are known to us from seal impressions found in Syria, Palestine, and Mesopotamia.[4] In Egypt, as well as in Israel, the relationship between god(dess) and mortal can be expressed in reciprocal terms: "I love," says Wisdom, "those who love me."[5]

It is evident that the notion of a "goddess of the king," which was part of a widespread royal ideology, was also familiar in Israel and played a part in shaping the image of wisdom in Proverbs 8. In fact, Wisdom must have been the name, or one of the names, of the Israelite kings' divine patroness. No doubt the scribes and civil servants—"all who are responsible for order"— were proud of being counted among those who shared the ruler's responsibility and his divine election, not to forget his divinely granted riches.

A more recent author has chosen the topic "The King and Divine Wisdom" for more detailed development. Chapters 6–9 of the book of Wisdom dating from the first century B.C. or A.D., are designed as a speech by King Solomon to his royal colleagues. Although in this text Wisdom—here called Sophia—is strictly subordinated to the God of Israel, her divine nature is still fairly evident. Wisdom is with God, and God sends her to humankind, beginning with kings. God has given power to the kings,[6] and he gives them Wisdom as their beloved consort, helper, and protectress. Here, too, echoes of the "goddess of kings"—primarily of Isis—can be discerned. Kloppenborg explains:

> According to the logic of Egyptian royal ideology, the Isis who saved Horus from danger and brought about his accession to the throne, the same Isis who is the associate of Re in creating and regulating the cosmos, is also the spouse of the

61

earthly king, conferring upon him the power to regulate human affairs.[7]

It is this logic that pseudo-Solomon borrows for his Sophia in order to make her an attractive rival of pagan Isis.

WISDOM AS WITNESS OF CREATION

Israelite sources present the Creator as the architect and master builder of the world. He set the earth on its foundations, established the mountains, and stretched out the heavens like a tent. Since we know only traces of this myth, and no contiguous narrative exists anywhere, we have no clear picture of the individual works of creation or their precise sequence. It seems clear, however, that one form of the myth included the Creator's victory over the untamed powers of the ocean. Not until the sea monster has been defeated and the waters have been given their limits can the work of creation be completed.[8]

How Proverbs 8 refers to the process of creation is no different from the general Israelite view. As the master builder,[9] the Creator formed the arch or tent of the heavens, made firm the clouds of the skies, fixed the sea below the earth, and assigned the waters their limits. How the Creator dealt with the waters cannot be spoken of in purely architectural terms. On the one hand, he drew a circle or horizon "on the face of the sea," marking the outer limit of the waters, where heaven and earth meet or, as Job 26:10, RSV, has it, "at the boundary between light and darkness."[10] On the other hand, when the Creator established a border between the land and the sea that surrounds it, he gave a command that the Sea should not transgress. The personal terms used for the Creator's dealings with the Sea at the border between land and water reflect how Israelites encountered the sea at the shore. It is here that the Sea can become an enemy and a monster that has to be fought against and "confined." The text echoes the ancient myth that explains how the Creator dealt with the conquered Sea Monster. By establishing a boundary to the Sea's legitimate sphere of activity, he gave him a place of his own and thus incorporated him into the ordered world.

62

Figure 5. Babylonian map of the world. According to ancient Near Eastern geography and myth, here represented on a sixth-century B.C. clay tablet, the earth is a flat disk surrounded by the sea. The Sea's legitimate sphere of existence is between the outer circle (i.e., the "horizon" the Creator drew on the face of the water) and the inner circle representing the boundary between land and sea.

Even before the creation of the world, Wisdom had come into being. She is older than all things. She is not the product of the artisan's skill, nor has she been conquered in battle to be made part of the ordered world. Rather, she has been *born* or brought forth by birth. Wisdom says of herself, "I was born *(ḥolalti)*," an expression used to refer to human birth. "Behold, I was brought forth (or born, *ḥolalti*) in iniquity," says one psalmist, "and in sin did my mother conceive me [Ps. 51:7, RSV]." Two other verbs are used to describe the origin of Wisdom: *qanah* and *nasak*. Although both terms have given commentators considerable headaches,[11] it seems that the most natural interpretation would be to relate these two verbs to the process of birth too. Whereas *qanani*

63

means "he has begotten me,"[12] *nesakkoti* (vocalized thus, instead of *nissakti*) must be rendered "I was fashioned [in the womb]."[13] Wisdom's father is none other than the Creator himself.

Not only from the point of view of orthodox early-Jewish belief is Wisdom, as Yahweh's daughter, a somewhat problematic figure. Scholars of comparative religion have their problems with her too. The original Canaanite creator deity was El rather than Yahweh, and we have no conclusive evidence for Yahweh as the creator god dating from before 594 B.C., when Jeremiah claimed for Yahweh what others claimed for the Mesopotamian creator god, Marduk.[14] Assuming that Proverbs 8 in its original version dates from a much earlier period, we may suggest that the name of Yahweh in the present text has replaced the original name of El.[15] The tablets found in ancient Ugarit have not revealed any cosmogonic myth, but scholars agree that El was held to be the creator, pointing out that more recent Semitic inscriptions make mention of "El, creator of the earth," a phrase virtually identical with the biblical "El Elyon, the creator of heaven and earth."[16]

Now El's consort, Athirat, is well known from Ugaritic texts as "mother of the gods" or "creatrix of the gods."[17] She may indeed be Wisdom's mother. There is another possibility, however. Within religious history there are several gods without mothers, and Wisdom may belong to these. The Greek goddess Athena, for instance, is the daughter of Zeus, but she has no mother. In mythical parlance this is represented by saying that Athena sprang from Zeus's forehead, and Pindar adds to this information, given by Hesiod, that Hephaestus had struck open the head with an axe. Similarly, the Egyptian god Thoth, himself inventor of the hieroglyphs and therefore related to writing, sprang from the head of Seth, in this case because Seth involuntarily had swallowed the semen of Horus. Or, to quote from the Egyptian Coffin Texts: "I am Shu, son of Atum; he fashioned me in his nose and I issued from his nostrils."[18] Such paradoxical phenomena are labeled "male pregnancy" and "male birth," ideas not entirely foreign to the Bible. One can refer to the creation myth according to which Eve was taken from within a man's, Adam's, body. Concerning Wisdom, the relevant idea may perhaps be understood from Sirach 24:3, although this is a much

64

later text, dating from around 200 B.C. According to this passage, Wisdom came forth from the mouth of God. One can never be quite sure about the details of Israel's lost polytheistic mythology. Interestingly, wisdom is not alien to the Ugaritic god El, "the wise" being one of his common epithets.[19]

What does it mean to say that Wisdom had been born before the Creator had made the world and that she was present at the creation? The answer to this question is not dependent on who the Creator was, but on how we understand the controversial verse 30a. Apart from obviously misguided constructions and proposed textual emendations, there are five debatable translations:

1. I was at his side as an *infant*.
2. I was at his side as a *confidant*.
3. I was at his side as *master builder* (or architect).
4. I was at his side as *counselor*.
5. I was at the side of the *master builder*.[20]

In each instance, the italicized term is an attempt to render the otherwise unattested Hebrew word *'amon*. The root of the term, *aleph—mem—nun*, is ambiguous. Just as unclear as the meaning of *'amon* is its position in the syntax. Does *'amon* refer to Wisdom or, as assumed by suggestion 5, to the Creator? Syntactically and etymologically, all the above translations can be supported. It seems, however, that the first and the last of the translations quoted are more viable than the others. Either the Creator is designated a master builder or Wisdom as a child. Neither reading adds new information to the text, and both, therefore, fit easily into the context. There is ample support for the notion that the Creator is the master builder of the world. The birth of Wisdom also goes well with the reading of Wisdom as a child. There are good reasons, however, in favor of translating "child," "ward," or "infant":

—The translation "infant" has a longer exegetical tradition, whereas the rendering "master builder" is a more recent conjecture.
—What is supposed to be the second biblical instance of *'amon* should be translated not as "master builder,

65

craftsman," but following the Akkadian *ummanu,* as "army."[21] Thus the "master builder" version loses considerable support.

—The translation "infant" is further supported by the terms *meśaheqet,* "(she is) frolicking," and *sha^cashu^cim,* "delight." Both terms can be used with reference to children.[22]

—Finally, the translation "infant" or "ward" fits in with Wisdom's proud self-presentation. Former pages of the Egyptian court were fond of using the title "ward of the king"[23] in order to advertise that they grew up with the king's sons and had therefore had an excellent educational background. The Bible has preserved the boastful words of an Egyptian official who is able to claim something similar, viz., to have had excellent teachers: "I am a son [student] of the wise, a son of ancient kings [Isa. 19:11, RSV]." The reference to ancient kings suggests that at school the official had studied instruction books that were written by, or attributed to, Egyptian kings.

Consequently, verse 30 should be understood as follows: Wisdom is the child of the Creator. She is a noble ward, a princess. As the Creator's pupil she watches the establishment of the world and learns the secrets of the universe. At the same time the Creator cares for his ward like a nursemaid. The *personal* categories that distinguish Wisdom's birth from the building process of creation are continued. We may therefore paraphrase verse 30a by saying, "I was beside him as an infant whom he (the Creator) has nursed." The Creator has a special love for Wisdom.

Wisdom, not the Creator and his work, is the central theme and focus of the poem. Only for her sake does the poem speak of creation. Yet she has no active part in creating the world; she is just a spectator. The beginning and end of Proverbs 8:27–30 are clear about this: "When he set the heavens into place, I was there . . . I was at his side as an infant." What is the meaning of Wisdom's presence as a witness of creation?

Following the lead indicated by an Egyptian title of honor and nobility, "ward of the king," I have suggested that there is an element of education and learning. This view can be supported and elucidated by two texts from other biblical books, one from the (Greek) book of Wisdom, the other from the book of Job. A third text quoted from is found in a Qumran scroll. The book of Wisdom is well aware that Wisdom was a witness at creation and that her presence there has given her superior and superhuman knowledge:

> *Wisdom is with you [God], she knows your works,*
> *For she was present when you made the world;*
> *She understands what is pleasing in your eyes.*
>
> —*Wisdom 9:9*

In the book of Wisdom, superhuman knowledge refers to that which is pleasing in the sight of God (i.e., it encompasses the ethical). The book of Job sees things differently. When Job wants God to justify what he has done (in sending misfortune and suffering to the innocent), God questions him roughly:

> *Where were you when I laid the foundation of the earth?*
> *Tell me, if you have understanding.*
> *Who determined its measurements[?]* . . .
> *Where is the way of the dwelling of light,*
> *and where is the place of darkness?* . . .
> *You know, for you were born then,*
> *and the number of your days is great!*
>
> —*Job 38:4–5, 19, 21,* RSV

The passage ends with an ironical note on human ignorance being caused by the distance in time between our birth and the days of creation. Any possible presence of human beings at creation is precluded. It follows that no one can understand all the mysteries of the created world and that, basically, no one is exalted over another. When Yukahainen, in the Finnish epic, boasts of his presence at the creation of the heavens and of his vast understanding of the inner workings of the universe, the theme of our biblical texts has been perverted.[24] Only Wisdom herself may boast of having been present at creation.

Additional evidence for the unique possibility of acquiring knowledge at the time of creation comes from a noncanonical psalm, found in a scroll from Qumran cave no. 11. The relevant passage is as follows:

> *Separating light from deep darkness*
> *By the knowledge of his mind he established the dawn.*
> *When all his angels had witnessed it they sang aloud,*
> For he showed them what they had not known:
> *Crowning the hills with fruit,*
> *Good food for every living being.*
> *Blessed be he who makes the earth by his power,*
> *Establishing the world in his wisdom.*[25]

Witnessing creation, the angels acquired knowledge, "for he [the Creator] showed them what they had not known." The time of creation is the privileged time for learning.

When we read Proverbs 8 in the light of the three texts quoted, it turns out that Wisdom must indeed have knowledge of all the secrets of the universe. The Job text lists some of these secrets, asking about measurements, light, darkness, snow, rain, stars, lightning, clouds, and so on. The Israelite teachers did not infer from the absence of a human witness at creation that nature was therefore simply unintelligible, beyond human comprehension, but they were well aware that nature has irresolvable secrets. In any case, in Proverbs 8, Wisdom provides vivid testimony that the ancient teachers felt quite proud of how close they had come to nature's mysteries. Wisdom, watching the Creator fashion the world, is an exalted image of the teacher observing nature and demonstrating to his students the wonders of creation.

This "nature wisdom," as it has been called, is implied when it is said of King Solomon: "He also uttered three thousand proverbs; and his songs were a thousand and five. He spoke of trees, from the cedar that is in Lebanon to the hyssop that grows out of the wall; he spoke also of beasts, and of birds, and of reptiles, and of fish [1 Kings 4:32–33, RSV]." The older view, according to which Solomon was considered to be the traditional author of fables, in which animals and plants play roles, has now been

68

abandoned by most scholars. They rightly prefer Albrecht Alt's view,[26] which suggests that Solomon's wisdom did not refer to the creation of moralizing, but of "academic" literature. The extrabiblical specimen of this genre that Alt refers to is the *Onomasticon of Amenope,* an Egyptian text dating from around 1100 B.C. This writing is a list enumerating beings and things of the heavens, the waters, and the earth; of divine and royal persons, courtiers, officers, professions, classes, tribes, and types of people (including those outside Egypt); of Egyptian cities; of buildings and their parts; of estates; of types of grain and their products; of food and drink; of parts of the ox and kinds of meat—altogether 610 entries preserved, without even reaching the end of the piece in its original length. While having an obviously practical function for apprentice scribes, the work also constitutes an early version of an encyclopedia, be it only in the form of a list of key words. It is especially worth noting that the title identifies the work as an "instruction," using a term that normally refers to collections of moral injunctions and practical maxims. Amenope's preface gives his encyclopedic list a mythical background:

> Beginning of the teaching for clearing the mind, for instruction of the ignorant and for learning all things that exist: what Ptah created, what Thoth copied down, heaven with its affairs, earth and what is in it, what the mountains belch forth, what is watered by the flood [of the Nile], all that is grown on the back of earth, excogitated by the scribe of the sacred books in the House of Life, Amenope, son of Amenope.[27]

What Amenope in a unique intellectual effort recorded is basically identical with Thoth's blueprint and transcript of creation. The scholar-cum-scribe Amenope reconstructed, as it were, the original list compiled by the patron deity of scribes. The underlying idea is somewhat similar to a theological commonplace generally attributed to astronomer Kepler: the scientist, by scrutinizing and discovering the laws of nature, reconstructs "the Creator's secret thoughts."

Like their Egyptian colleague, the teachers of Israel traced everything natural and social they encountered back to creation. For them, Wisdom, their divine patroness, bridged the vast distance between the present day and what had happened in the beginning. Because of her mediating role, teachers can furnish their sometimes quite pedestrian, dry, and moralizing wisdom with the spark of myth.

Can we agree, then, with Wildeboer's often-repeated assertion that "Wisdom, in order to get a hearing, has to provide a new basis of motivation. So she shows her patent of nobility"?[28] Notwithstanding Wisdom's noble descent (from God) and her venerable age, it is her presence at creation that ultimately counts. Among the sages of Israel, age does indeed matter, but what counts even more is wisdom gained by observation and application of the intellect.[29] If we were to correct Wildeboer's witty statement, we would have to exchange the patent of nobility for a doctor's degree. Of course, Wisdom would not have to work for her doctorate like anyone else. As a person of nobility, she had the unique privilege of being present at creation and thus could playfully penetrate the secrets of the universe. What others have to study came to her quite naturally. She is Wisdom herself!

CHAPTER 9

Brief Commentary on Proverbs 8:1–36

The poem opens by introducing the speaker and setting the scene:

> 1   *It is[1] [Lady] Wisdom calling*
>   *[Lady] Understanding raising her voice.*
> 2   *On the walls[2] [of the city], on the paths,*
>   *In the streets she takes her stand,*
> 3   *Beside the gates, at the entrance of the city,*
>   *At the portals she chants.*

It has already been shown in the discussion of Proverbs 1 that Wisdom selects places in which orators look for an audience, merchants for customers, and, of course, teachers for students. After the scene has been set, Wisdom begins her speech. In keeping with the rules of rhetoric, the speech opens with an address:

> 4   *"To you, O men, I appeal,*
>   *My speech is for [all] the sons of men!"*

This address creates the impression of a huge crowd listening to the speaker. Similar forms of address, however, make us suspect that this is an illusion. "Hear this, all peoples! Give ear, all inhabitants of the world, both low and high, rich and poor

71

together [Ps. 49:1–2, RSV]," says one orator, and another one, although slightly more modest, speaks with a similar voice: "Hear this, you aged men, give ear, all inhabitants of the land [Joel 1:2, RSV]!" In all these cases the speaker talks to just a small audience. To imply and implore, in the opening summons, a larger circle of hearers has the effect of emphasizing the universal validity of what is being said. "The writer," asserts Sartre, speaking of *any* writer, "basically addresses *all* men."[3] This is shown quite clearly by the second quotation. Here a prophet's immediate audience seems to be the elders who are leaders in social and political life. Probably many elders were present when the oracle was uttered. Because the message is valid and meaningful to all, the speaker rhetorically addresses "all inhabitants of the land." In the same vein the psalmist, when speaking to a congregation, can appeal to "all nations" to praise Yahweh.[4]

Following her opening address, Wisdom exhorts her audience to acquire knowledge. Then she extols her teachings in glowing terms:

> 5   *O immature ones, learn shrewdness,*
>   *O foolish ones, instruct [your] minds!*
> 6   *Listen! I speak [teach] noble things,*[5]
>   *And from my lips comes what is right;*
> 7   *What my mouth utters is reliable.*
>   *Wickedness is abhorrent to my lips.*
> 8   *All the words of my mouth are just,*
>   *None of them perverse or crooked;*
> 9   *All are straight[forward] to him who is intelligent*
>   *And right to those who have attained knowledge.*
> 10 *Prefer my instruction to silver*
>   *And knowledge to the finest gold!*
> 11 *For wisdom is better than [red] coral,*
>   *No jewels can compare with her.*

Obviously, Wisdom uses didactic language. Untutored young men are asked to acquire shrewdness (i.e., practical wisdom). This, of course, is the fundamental objective of the school, as the preface to Proverbs 1—9 explains.[6] Everything else Wisdom says serves to enhance and support her basic challenge. "Listen, I speak," she says, referring to her lectures. The principal method of instruction is the lecture or probably the dictation of texts such as didactic, moralistic discourses like the ones preserved in Proverbs 1—7. With regard to its moral quality, the teacher praises her instruction as noble, right, reliable, just, with nothing twisted or crooked in it. Finally, instruction is recommended to "those who have attained knowledge" (i.e., those who have already made progress in learning). This gain corresponds to the advice given to advanced learners in the preface.[7] The closing verse of the section under consideration is a competitive aphorism that praises the value of wisdom as superior to precious material goods.

In the section to follow, Wisdom moves from praising the qualities of her teaching to praising herself as a heavenly, divine being. Her self-presentation is in three parts. First, she speaks of herself as a queen possessing all the virtues and powers of royalty (vss. 12–14); then she tells of her close ties with those in power on earth, who indeed depend on her (vss. 15–21); and finally, she explains her relationship to the Creator, whose daughter she is and whose construction work she has witnessed in person (vss. 22–31).

Wisdom is endowed with the full range of divine and royal powers:

> 12 *I am [Lady] Wisdom. I am shrewd,[8]*
> *I have attained much skill.*
> 13 *To fear Yahweh is to hate evil.*
> *Pride, arrogance, and the evil way*
> *And perverted speech: [these] I hate.*
> 14 *I know how to plan and to execute plans,*
> *I have insight, I am mighty.*

It seems that verse 13a, "To fear Yahweh is to hate evil," is a secondary addition to the original poem.[9] The gloss upsets the style by making verse 13 a unit consisting of three lines instead of two. Unlike the rest of the text, it is a statement in the third person rather than a proud assertion in the first. Obviously, a postexilic pious scribe incorporated a line he associated with "hate" and "evil."

What Wisdom boasts of can be reduced to three basic categories. She has intellectual capabilities—shrewdness, finesse, the ability to make plans *(ᶜeṣah)*, insight, and, of course, wisdom *(ḥokmah);* she has moral qualities—she hates pride, arrogance, and perverted speech; and she has power *(geburah, tushiyah)*. Some of the Hebrew terms that are used require explanation. The word ᶜeṣah, often rendered as "counsel," is "the political planning which goes into policy-making."[10] The test of ᶜeṣah, therefore, is the degree of success that it achieves when put into operation. "So there is little profit in spending time over ᶜeṣah," explains McKane, "unless one possesses *geburah* [power] to give effect to it. Hence it is an activity proper to men who *really* have power and responsibility."[11] *Geburah* refers to military prowess or valor and, at a more individual level, to the strength necessary to prevail over an adversary, for instance.[12]

Real power and responsibility, in the ancient East, rest with the gods and kings, and it is not surprising, therefore, to find both Yahweh and the idealized Israelite king furnished with the same qualities: wisdom, moral insight (and action), and power.[13] Some outstanding biblical personalities, like the young David and the perfect woman of Proverbs 31, are also reported to combine intellectual qualities with strength. Daniel, too, possessed both wisdom and strength, and he had as companions young men who were "skilful in wisdom" as well as "endowed with vigor."[14] As Caquot has pointed out, the union of wisdom and strength in one person represents, for Israelite culture, the very image of an ideal person.

In both practical and political life, wisdom and strength or power are not often found together. The sages are often without power, and the powerful are rarely wise. Plato's republic, in which political leadership was to be with the sages, is strictly utopian, and philosopher-kings, like the Roman emperor Marcus Aurelius (second century A.D.), were rarely successful. "There is a most natural reason for this," explains Caquot. "Whatever its field of application may be, wisdom is improvable; it is the fruit of experience; thus it ripens with age, and it is common to identify *wise* with *old* and wisdom with grey hair."[15] Bodily strength and ardor in combat, however, are the domain of youth. Each age range has its virtue, and one cannot have the benefits of both old age and youth at the same time.

Wisdom, endowed with intellectual qualities as well as with power, ranks higher than the kings of this earth. In fact, it is she who allows mortal men to be rulers:

> 15 *Through me kings reign*
> *And rulers issue just decrees.*
> 16 *Through me officials do their work,*
> *Noble men and all who are responsible for order.*

The three terms, *kings* (and rulers), *officials,* and *nobles,* designate the people who, in a political and social sense, constitute authority for the Israelite. Besides the king and his court officials, there were the nobles or notables, the heads of wealthy and influential families whom the Arabs call sheiks. To these men one listens, and they may be defined as "those who are socially and morally held in esteem." In the time of the Hebrew monarchy the leading men of a city or village formed a council that regulated the affairs of the community. Together with the officials of the royal court, these nobles formed the ruling class. Using Max Weber's terminology, one can say that what we have here is a combination of gerontocracy and sultanism; both of these come under the general heading of "traditional authority." In a society ruled by traditional authorities, the right to make decisions in public affairs and to exercise power is claimed "on the basis of the sanctity of the order and the attendant powers of control as they have been handed down from the past, 'have always existed.'" To this, Weber adds that in such a society a feeling of loyalty would typically be "cultivated through a common process of education."[16] As a school text, Proverbs 8 is a document of this educational process that inculcated and cemented loyalty. The reason why court officials and nobles are mentioned here along with the king is easily imaginable: the poem was written by a teacher at the school in which these people received their professional training. The passage reveals the considerable self-esteem of officials and sheiks who exercised their office not just in the name of the king (which would actually be true for officials), but in the name of Wisdom herself, to whom even the king is subject and must bow.

The passage immediately following describes more closely the relationship between Wisdom and those who hold positions of public authority:

> 17 *Those who love* me *I love*
> *And those who seek me will find me.*
> 18 *Immeasurable riches[17] are with me,*
> *Choice treasures and prosperity.*
> 19 *My fruit is better than fine gold,*
> *My produce better than choice silver.*
> 20 *I walk on the way of order,*
> *Along the paths of justice,*
> 21 *Endowing with wealth those who love me,*
> *Filling their treasures.*

The terms love—seek—find are often used to describe relationships between God and human individuals, between man and woman, and between the student and knowledge.[18] This kind of vocabulary conjures up a host of associations. Yet the relationship between Wisdom and those who maintain order in society must be understood primarily as a bond of loyalty. Ancient Near Eastern texts, including the Bible, refer to this kind of bond as a bond of "love," a term that should not be overloaded with connotations of romantic sentiment, friendship, and affection. It means simply loyalty.[19]

Those who win Wisdom's "love" gain great wealth, granted by the goddess. Treasures, of course, are never given away without merit, but only as a reward for just conduct. The poem plays with the Hebrew terms *ṣedeq* and *ṣedaqah* in a subtle way that cannot be reproduced in translation. "Prosperity" (vs. 18) is *ṣedaqah*, but the "order" (vs. 20) maintained by authorities is also *ṣedaqah;* in verses 15 and 16 *ṣedeq* is used in reference to "just" decrees and those who are responsible for "order." The concept must be seen in the light of a just and ultimately beneficial order of both creation and society.[20] To render the breadth of this perspective in a single English term is impossible.

Having spoken of her love for rulers, whom she has chosen, in

76

the previous section, Wisdom now turns to a new subject: her relationship to the creator god and his creation. The Septuagint inserts two lines to make the transition less abrupt: "If I declare to you the things that daily happen, I will remember also to recount the things of old." First, Wisdom tells of her existence before creation:

> 22 *Yahweh [originally, El?] begot me when he began to be*
> *active [literally, at the beginning of his way],*
> *In the earliest days of his creation, long ago.*
> 23 *Ages ago he fashioned me [in the womb],*
> *At the beginning, at the origin of earth.*
> 24 *There was still no sea*
> *Full of water when I was born.*
> 25 *Before [the foundations of] the mountains were sunk,*
> *Before the hills I was born,*
> 26 *When he had not yet made earth and fields,*
> *Or the world's first clump of clay.*

Wisdom does not tell of her existence before creation in a simple, straightforward statement, but with a great display of rhetoric. Six terms are used to indicate her existence before creation: at the beginning of the Creator's course, in the earliest days of his creation, long ago, ages ago, at the beginning, at the origin of earth. Wisdom, instead of belonging to the "days of old," to the primeval entities of creation, was begotten *before* the world was built. That is why she was able to be present at the actual process of creation of which she is not simply a part. She belongs to the world before creation, a world that can only be referred to in negative terms: when there was no sea, before the foundations of the mountains were sunk, before the Creator had made hills, earth, and fields.

The poet does not leave it at this, but makes the difference between creation and Wisdom even more explicit. Besides giving her precedence in time, he also uses a special vocabulary to draw the distinction. While the creation of the material world can be referred to in terms of craftsmanship and building activities (vss. 27ff.), Wisdom's creation must be spoken of in personal terms: Wisdom was "begotten," "fashioned" (as in the womb), and eventually "born." Gods are not created as the world is created; they are begotten and born, not made. There is a qualitative difference between gods and the realm of the created.

In the passage that follows the poet moves from the account of Wisdom's preexistence to a report on the Creator's work of creation.

> 27 *When he set the heavens into place I was there,*
> *When he drew a circle on the face of the sea;*
> 28 *When he made firm the clouds above,*
> *And fixed the fountains and the sea [below];*
> 29 *When he assigned the sea its limits*
> *So that the waters never transgress his command;*
> *When he marked out the foundations of the earth—*
> 30 *Then I was at his side as an infant.*

The Creator is pictured as a builder and an architect. As a master craftsman he builds the vault or tent of the sky, fashions a firm cover of clouds, and draws the circle of the horizon around the primal sea. He fixes the sea and assigns limits to the waters. This done, the dry land can emerge and become visible, and the Creator is able to mark the foundations of the earth. As the Creator is finishing his work, Wisdom, who is still a child, is present and, by watching him, gains insight into the secrets of the cosmos. Precisely because of this she is far superior to all human beings, who are straining to put together what limited knowledge of nature and creation they may gather.

Although Wisdom's superiority has been demonstrated, the passage still does not close with verse 30a. Up to this point only Wisdom's presence has been referred to. The author now goes on to state what she has been doing:

> 30 *[His] delight day by day,*
> *Frolicking before him at all times,*
> 31 *Frolicking on his earth,*
> *Delighting in the sons of men.*

On the morning of creation, Wisdom is still a little child who plays and frolics around. Happy play is her first expression of

78

life. There is a nice parallel to this in Egyptian mythology. In the Bremner-Rhind papyrus the creator god reports that "I came into being in this land and Shu and Tefenet rejoiced in the Nun [sea] in which they were."[21] On the morning of creation the god's children are happily playing in the ocean. Joy is their first expression of life. We can also compare this with the legendary laughter of Zoroaster on the very day he was born.[22] Keel has pointed out that joyful play in the presence of the Creator is an unmistakable sign of intimacy. Only someone who belongs to the family may play, laugh, and frolic around in the presence of the head of an oriental household.[23] Some authors have made the child's innocent play in the Creator's presence into a liturgical act[24] or related it to a biblical tradition that the creation was completed "when the morning stars sang together and all the sons of God shouted for joy."[25] This, however, is getting us away from the original image. The poem knows nothing of Wisdom's liturgy or heavenly song.

Wisdom, then, is the Creator's healthy child, displaying her joy and energy. By referring to her frolicking and cheerful play, the goddess also softens the air of authority that dominates the rest of her discourse.

It is not without significance *where* the divine child plays. Her playground is the earth, the place inhabited by men and women. Her first playground continues to be the realm where Wisdom exercises her authority. There is, perhaps, a hint of her mediating position between the Creator and humankind—a role quite befitting a minor goddess who happens to be the Creator's daughter. At any rate the reference to the "sons of men" provides an apt transition to what follows (viz., Wisdom's final appeal to her pupils).

At the end of her speech Wisdom returns to her initial role as a teacher. In a final plea she punctuates her instruction by offering more reasons for the student to listen and learn. Again, she uses didactic speech:

> 32 *Now, sons, listen to me!*
> *Happy are they who keep my ways!*
> 33 *Listen to [my] instruction and become wise![26]*
> *Do not spurn [it]![27]*

³⁴ *Happy is the man who listens to me,*
    Standing at my door day by day,
    Waiting [for me] at my threshold!
³⁵ *For* he who acquires me attains[28] *life*
    And obtains favor from Yahweh [originally, from the
    gods?].
³⁶ *But he who misses me, hurts himself;*
    All who hate me love death [originally, love Mot].

Once again we find here the common forms and motifs of sapiential language: the macarism,[29] the challenge to acquire and not to reject wisdom,[30] the student's unwillingness to learn and his hate of the teacher,[31] and, eventually, the willing student who chooses wisdom and thus finds life (i.e., happiness, prosperity, and success).[32] The good student waits beside the teacher's house.[33] Unfortunately, the text does not tell us whether the lesson is held *in* the house (with the student waiting for the classroom or lecture hall to be opened) or whether, eager to learn, the student waits for the teacher to come out of his house so that the lesson may begin outside. Since the first reference that seems to imply regular instruction in a building is of much later date,[34] we cannot tell whether the poem thinks of teachers conducting classes in their homes.

Whatever the case may be, students are expected to report to their teacher early in the morning. "See, who is a man of prudence," suggests Sirach; "seek him out [early in the morning]; let your feet wear away his doorstep."[35] Proverbs 8:34 praises the student who is overpunctual in attending his lessons. In an age that lacked precise ways of measuring hours and a culture that did not share our modern sense of time shaped by our world of work, punctuality seems to have been a rare virtue. In the third century A.D., Rabbi Yohanan lists "visiting the house of instruction early in the morning" among those works that, like hospitality, visiting the sick, and devotion in prayer, are profitable in this world as well as in the world to come.[36]

The concluding lines (vss. 35–36) offer a "summary appraisal." Wisdom is again related to a god called Yahweh. No doubt this refers back to the mythological section, an intended reference to the Creator. Originally, however, the formula "to find favor from Yahweh" may have been "to find favor from *the gods ('elohim).*" The gods have been replaced by Yahweh in an attempt to make the poem acceptable to Yahweh-aloneists of the postexilic period.[37] There is only one instance in which the revision did not remove the gods from the text of Proverbs 1—9, and the relevant passage has indeed some similarity to ours: "so you will find favor and good repute in the sight of gods *('elohim)* and men."[38]

The contrast between life and death is a fitting theme for the closing line of the poem. The preceding chapter, Proverbs 7, ends with the same word, death. Death, for the polytheist reader of preexilic Israel, was, of course, the god Mot (i.e., Death), a divinity well known from the texts of Ugarit. As a celestial goddess of life, Wisdom is opposed to Mot, whose realm is the nether world. Mot, however, can extend his kingdom into the world of the living. He reigns where people fail to listen to Wisdom and thus fail to live in the full sense of the term. Life and death stand for ultimate success and final failure. This is what wisdom is all about.

PART THREE

LADY WISDOM VS. LADY FOLLY

(Proverbs 9)

The Poem Proverbs 9:1–18

1   *When [Lady] Wisdom had built a house,*
    Had hewn seven pillars,
2   *She slaughtered, spiced the wine,*
    And set the table.
3   *She sent out the maids to call*
    From the walls of the city:
4   *"Whoever is immature, let him enter here!"*
    To him who is without learning she says,
5   *"Come, eat my food,*
    And drink the wine I have spiced!
6   *Get away from the immature, and live!*
    Get on the way of understanding!

7   *Whoever [tries to] instruct a mischief-maker, earns abuse,*
    And the teacher of a wicked man [retains] a stigma.
8   *Do not teach a mischief-maker, or he will hate you,*
    Instruct a knowledgeable man and he will love you.
9   *Give instruction to a knowledgeable man, and he will*
    grow wiser,
    Teach an orderly person, and he will gain in learning.
10 *The beginning of wisdom is the fear of Yahweh [orig-*
    inally, fear of the gods?],
    And knowledge of the Holy One[s] is [true] understand-
    ing.

11 *For through me your days will increase,*
    Your [happy] years will be many.
12 *If you are wise, you are wise for your own [benefit];*
    If you are a mischief-maker—you bear it alone."
13 *Lady Folly bustles about.*
    Knowing seduction and nothing else,
14 *She places herself at the entrance of her house,*
    [Using] the city wall as a chair,
15 *In order to call those who pass by*
    Keeping straight their paths:
16 *"Whoever is immature, let him enter here!"*
    To him who is without learning she says,
17 *"Stolen water is sweet,*
    And bread [gotten] in secret is tasty."
18 *Yet he does not know that the Rephaïm are there,*
    That her guests are in the depth of Sheol.

A fitting title for this poem might be "An Invitation Addressed to Young Men." There are actually two invitations: one by Lady Wisdom and another by Lady Folly. Wisdom and Folly are the two powers vying for favor with students. There is general agreement on this among commentators. The agreement stops here, however. The poem raises all kinds of questions. For example, many authors consider verses 7–12, or part of it, to be a later interpolation disturbing the original text. Which are the interpolated lines, and how do we account for their presence? Folly is not only a problematic figure in ancient teachers' minds. Modern scholars also want to know more about her identity. Is she another goddess or just a city prostitute plying her trade? Wisdom, for her part, is probably less problematic. Yet there are the mysterious seven columns of her house that have been given various and quite unconvincing interpretations. The first question that has to be dealt with is the interpolation. Once the intrusive section has been removed, we can look at the poem itself.

CHAPTER 11

A Textual Intrusion: Proverbs 9:7–10

Following Proverbs 9:6 one would expect a continuation of Wisdom's invitation or, as an alternative, an introduction of her rival, Folly. Instead, there are a few lines about the teacher and teaching, in what are now verses 7–9. After verse 10 comes a motto on the fear of Yahweh, standing by itself. Then, Wisdom's invitation is resumed and ends with verse 12. Although the Hebrew text quite logically proceeds with Folly, the Septuagint inserts several additional lines:

> He who stays himself upon falsehoods,
> Attempts to rule the winds,
> And the same will pursue birds in their flight:
> For he has forsaken the ways of his own vineyard,
> And has caused the axles of his own husbandry to go astray;
> And he goes through a dry desert,
> And a land appointed to drought,
> And he gathers barrenness with his hands.

The insertions break the unity of the original poem to such an extent that the proper association of its parts is no longer recognizable. For the reader of the Septuagint version in particular, Proverbs 9:13 is the beginning of a new poem.

87

Because there is no manuscript evidence for the secondary character of verses 7–10, one can only speculate about the reasons for the insertion. As a tentative interpretation, the following hypothesis may be offered. It assumes that the original text, although consisting of the same material, was rearranged in the process of transmission. The original sequence must have been Proverbs 9:1–6, 11–18, 7–10. Later, verses 7–10 were transferred to their present position between verses 6 and 11. If we include the Septuagint in our consideration, the redactional process involves three stages:

Stage 1: Proverbs 9:1–6, 11–18, 7–10—reconstructed original text

Stage 2: Proverbs 9:1–6, *7–10*, 11–18—present Hebrew text

Stage 3: Proverbs 9:1–6, 7–10, 11–12, *additions*, 13–18, *additions*—Septuagint version

At Stage 1 the poem on Wisdom and Folly was followed by a new and independent passage that, at Stage 2, became verses 7–10. It stood at the end of Proverbs 1—9 and served as the concluding paragraph. At the end of the book the teacher is advised not to waste his energy on undisciplined and unpromising students. Verse 10 stands by itself, isolated: "The beginning of wisdom is the fear of Yahweh, and knowledge of the Holy One is understanding." This is a "motto," an emphatic closing sentence that refers back to a similar line in Proverbs 1:7.[1] The last sentence of the closing paragraph echoes the last line of the preface, thus rounding off the little sapiential book.

Both mottoes—Proverbs 1:7 and 9:10—may have been inserted by Yahweh-aloneists during the late monarchy or even later, but they could also date from much earlier.[2] If we assume that at one time, Yahweh was inserted to replace an earlier *'elohim*, verse 10 would read thus:[3]

The beginning of wisdom is the fear of the gods,
And knowledge of the holy ones is [true] understanding.

The expression "fear of the gods" is actually known from another biblical text, and scholars believe that there is something "international" about it. Without being specifically Israelite, it refers to "a certain respect and regard for the most elementary of social norms, whose severe guardian was known to be the deity."[4] The *qedoshim* of the second line, usually rendered "the Holy One" and understood as the one God, may in fact be translated as "the Holy Ones" and imply a multiplicity of deities.[5] This is how an Israelite polytheist would have read the passage.

An early copyist or reeditor of the Hebrew book of Proverbs, possibly one who used it as a textbook for students, found the end of his master copy in bad shape. Papyrus, the most common writing material in biblical times,[6] perishes easily. Possibly, the end of the papyrus scroll had become dry and brittle and had eventually dissolved into several fragments. When he reconstituted the text, he failed to understand verses 7–10 as the somewhat laconic conclusion of the book. By inserting them after verse 6 he created the distorted text we now find in our masoretic manuscripts as well as in the printed editions (Stage 2). Perhaps the redactor did not look for an actual conclusion because the book he edited or created did not end after the poem on Wisdom and Folly. Within the larger structure of the canonical book of Proverbs, chapters 1–9 serve as a kind of introduction. The end of this introduction did not necessarily need to be rounded off by a carefully crafted conclusion.

The Hebrew document available to the Greek translator, his *Vorlage*, already had verses 7–10 removed from the end of Proverbs 1—9. While the redactor who transposed verses 7–10 to their present position seems to have considered them as belonging to Wisdom's speech, the translator must have been unaware of this connection. His own insertions, placed after verse 12, contain material that is unrelated to either the original poem or the original closing paragraph.

If this reconstruction is accepted, we can read Proverbs 9:1–6, 11–18 as belonging together and forming a complete poem.[7] As a corollary, we can consider Proverbs 1—9 as an ancient Hebrew instruction book that is independent and complete in itself. That it became the first piece of a compilation of other didactic material that now forms the canonical book of Proverbs is another story. It became the introduction to this book but had not been compiled solely for this purpose.

CHAPTER 12

Invitation to a Banquet in a House of Seven Pillars

Now that we have removed verses 7–10 and thus recovered the original form of the poem, we may turn to Wisdom's invitation. It is an invitation to her house, which has obviously just been built and completed. For commentators, the most puzzling features of this house are its seven pillars. Ancient and modern authors alike have looked for a hidden or symbolic meaning in the number seven and have suggested the seven liberal arts of the medieval curriculum, the seven sacraments of the Catholic Church, the seven gifts of the Holy Spirit; or disregarding the number seven, they have spoken of apostles, patriarchs, and teachers on whom Christ has built his church as if on pillars. Critical commentators, abandoning the allegorical method, have referred to the seven planets that constitute the house of the universe, speculated about the function of columns in ancient ritual architecture, or resorted to a rigorous emendation of the text in order to get rid of the puzzling number seven.[1] The seven pillars of wisdom continue to be a problem. It seems that they have not yet betrayed their secret.

Strangely enough, commentators have never considered the use of pillars in the architecture of ancient Israelite urban dwellings. A standard design is the so-called four-room house in which three rooms surround a small, semiopen courtyard that forms the fourth room and presumably functioned as the main area for everyday activities. "An almost constant feature of Israelite houses," explains an archaeologist, "particularly those with four rooms, was monolithic stone pillars supporting the roof. The pillars, of square or rectangular section and fashioned from a single stone from one to two meters long, are characteristic of Israelite building in general."[2] Such pillars normally were used to support the roof covering half the inner court. The number of columns varies; although a standard design would have four pillars, one can find any number between three and eight. The dimensions of the house and the quality of construction depend on the financial resources of the owner, and these again depend on social status.

The Israeli archaeologist Yadin has found such a house with pillars, which he calls "the most beautifully planned and preserved of the Israelite structures at Hazor." When excavating ancient Hazor, it was the stone pillars protruding from the ground that first attracted his attention. "These soon proved to be a row of pillars in a court of a house," Yadin reports. "The house itself consisted of a large court, measuring 9 × 8 meters, with a series of rooms on two of its sides. The eastern part of the court was covered by a roof supported by six well-dressed, square, stone pillars, three of which were still found *in situ*."[3] The excavator believes that the location of the house right in the heart of the city indicates that it was owned by one of the wealthier citizens of eighth-century B.C. Hazor.

Houses of a similar design, with *seven* pillars, have actually been found.[4] Two were located in Hazor, dating from the eighth century. Another one, in Hirbet el-Mshash, dates from the eleventh century B.C. The building technique, the architectural design, and the use of pillars remained relatively uniform over the centuries. The narrow door of the eleventh-century B.C. house leads into a courtyard. Behind a wall, or half-wall, structured by seven pillars is the major room of the house, behind which there are two smaller rooms. All these rooms were covered by the roof. The biggest room seems not to have been completely closed off from the court. Probably a low sleeper wall supported the row of pillars, so that the main room was actually an aisled hall. Thus the seven columns were a visible structural element.

The author of our poem must have had such a design in mind

91

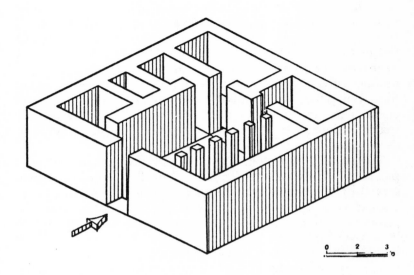

Figure 6. Axiometric view of an eighth-century B.C. pillared house in ancient Hazor excavated by Yigael Yadin.

when he wrote about Wisdom's house with seven pillars. The reference to *seven* pillars no doubt suggests an unusually spacious and elegant construction—the home of a patrician. An Arabic saying, on the use of pillars in the traditional farmhouse of Syria, can teach us why a reference to the extraordinary size of the house is quite appropriate for our poem. "In each of the old rooms," reports an anthropologist,

> are several pillars supporting the rafters. The number of pillars depends upon the size of the individual room. When, in former times, people praised someone as a wealthy man, they said: "His house rests on twelve pillars." This not only referred to the fact that he owns a big house, but also indicated that he is able to receive many guests there. Still today, the saying can be heard quite frequently.[5]

Receiving and entertaining guests are part of the obligatory lifestyle of a wealthy householder and are considered normal. A

92

sizable number of guests is evidence of what Thorstein Veblen has termed "conspicuous consumption"; it contributes to the social prestige of the upper classes. Anthropologists are well acquainted with the underlying connection between prestige, hospitality, and the consumption of goods. "In traditional societies," explains Ioan Lewis, "part of the price of power is the duty to dispense lavish and frequent hospitality, on a scale befitting one's rank, thus promoting redistributive consumption."[6] Thus even the poor and the powerless get their share. The wealthy have to follow the noblesse oblige maxim by inviting and entertaining guests more frequently than their less well-to-do neighbors.

Wisdom, who, as a goddess, is certainly a noble figure, owns a patrician house with seven pillars and is able to receive a large number of guests. It makes sense that the seven pillars of Wisdom's home are referred to in the context of her invitation to a lavish banquet.

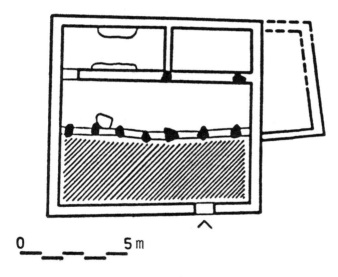

Figure 7. Eleventh-century B.C. house with seven pillars in Hirbet el-Mshash. The entrance leads into an open courtyard (shaded), which is separated from the rest of the house by a row of seven pillars.

Invitation to a Banquet

After a house—an individual's home, a temple, a royal palace, or any structure in the world of the gods—has been erected, it has to be inaugurated, and this is generally done at a festive banquet.

Our ancient sources tell us about national festivals, the distribution of food and drink, and lavish banquets at the inauguration of Solomon's temple, at its reinauguration under King Hezekiah, and on the completion of Assyrian palaces.[7] At the inauguration of the palace of Nimrud the entire population was invited to celebrate, and an inscription lists the large quantities of food, meat, and wine that were distributed.[8] Unfortunately, we can only speculate about the customs connected with the completion of an ordinary citizen's home. A law that postpones conscription on the grounds of having to inaugurate a home seems to imply that important social duties were included in the ceremony.[9] Among the Buaziz of Morocco, the owner of a newly built house had to slaughter a sheep and invite all the men and women of the village.[10] Probably the ancient Israelite's completion of a house involved similar obligations.

In mythology, we read of banquets at the dedication of the Babylonian god Marduk's palace[11] and of the Ugaritic god Baal's heavenly mansion. Here is part of the relevant Ugaritic text:

> Mightiest Baal did rejoice, (saying):
> "I have built my mansion of silver,
> My palace of gold."
> Baal put his mansion in order,
> Hadad did put his palace in order.
> He did slay oxen, also sheep,
> He did fell bulls and fatted rams,
> Yearling calves,
> Skipping lambs and kids.
> He did call his brothers into his mansion,
> His kinsfolk into the midst of his palace,
> He did call the seventy sons of Athirat.
> He did supply the gods with rams and with wine.
> He did supply the goddesses with ewes and with wine.[12]

Women, not only men, may invite guests on such occasions. The Assyrian queen Naqia, for instance, gave a banquet after she had built a palace in Nineveh for her son, King Asarhaddon.[13] In Hittite mythology the goddess Inaras invites and entertains a guest.[14] In a Ugaritic epic it is Huray, King Keret's spouse, who is the hostess, on one occasion. Although the relevant passage is severely mutilated and fragmentary, the following text could be recovered:

> *And the maiden Huray addressed them:*
> *"I have called you to eat and drink,*
> *And to make sacrifice for Keret your lord."* . . .
> *She slew the fattest of her fatlings,*
> *She opened tuns of wine.* . . .
> *She put forth her hand to the dish,*
> *She put a knife to the flesh.*
> *And the maiden Huray addressed them:*
> *"I have called you to eat and to drink."[15]*

We can see, then, that when Wisdom, as a goddess, invites guests to the dedication of her house, it is not an isolated occurrence in Near Eastern mythology. Did our poet borrow the scene of building the house (or palace) and sending out maids from some mythological or epic context? Unfortunately, there is no answer to this question. Practically all of Israel's polytheistic mythology has been lost.

EATING AS AN IMAGE

By verse 4, at the latest, the reader of the poem realizes that the invitation to the banquet is poetic imagery and that in reality it is concerned with school and learning. In verse 5 the reader is again reminded of the banquet. The poetic image (Wisdom's invitation to a banquet) and the corresponding reality (the teacher's invitation to attend his lessons) are placed side by side without being linked. The reader has to find out how and why image and reality are related. This is, of course, good poetry. One has to read "creatively"; it is precisely this that lends charm to the poetic imagery.

95

It is not difficult to guess at a reason for the juxtaposition of school and banquet. In the eyes of the poet, learning is as receptive a process as eating. "The ear tests words as the palate tastes food" is at least a partial explanation for the association of the two.[16] Eating, just like learning a lesson, has the connotation of taking something into oneself and assimilating it. The image suggests that the teacher offers spiritual food, food for the spirit. Yet this interpretation does not exhaust the image. Is not an invitation to learning as honorable as a banquet invitation? There is the prospect of table fellowship too. At school the student sits at the table sharing food with Wisdom. Is not being Wisdom's guest like being a god's guest in a temple, partaking of that god's table? Israelites seem to have understood the sacrificial meal as sitting at a deity's table and receiving divine blessings. Eating, especially in a ritual context, had a significant spiritual dimension.

The use of eating as a metaphor or image for learning in Proverbs 9 is not isolated in biblical literature. Jesus Sirach speaks of the thirst for wisdom and presents Wisdom as a woman who prepares the "bread of understanding" and "the water of learning" for her husband.[17] Perhaps the closest parallel to our passage is a summons to listen to a prophet's message, found in Second Isaiah. Here the prophet seems to imitate the oriental watersellers or breadsellers from the busy streets of Middle Eastern cities; like them, the prophet calls out, offering something for sale; unlike them, he takes no money for his message.[18]

In Folly's invitation in the second part of the poem the metaphor of eating is used again but takes on a different meaning. There, eating and drinking refer to illicit sexual contacts.

96

CHAPTER 13

Folly—a Harlot

Prostitution was known and practiced throughout the ancient world. As a profession, it had by no means the unsavory reputation that it has today. It was thought of differently in different places. Well-established brothels could even be found as institutions connected with and managed by temples. For a long time both female and male prostitutes had their dwellings within the precinct of the Jerusalem temple and practiced their trade there.[1] Perhaps similar institutions existed at the so-called High Places, but the evidence is not quite clear and may refer to orgiastic rituals rather than to paid prostitution.[2]

Older literature assumed ritual status for ancient Near Eastern prostitution, especially when it was linked to temples. Scholars believed that prostitutes were part of the official temple personnel; together with priests offering sacrifices, prophets who gave oracles, and temple musicians, they exercised what amounts to a priestly function. Traffic with these prostitutes was regarded as a form of worship or called fertility magic. Whoever had intercourse with a temple prostitute assumed power over the harlot and, by implication, over her goddess and thus was able to secure fertility for himself as well as for others. At any rate, this view was recently suggested by Andrew Greeley in *The Mary Myth*.[3] The whole idea of ritual prostitution, however, should be relegated to the category of fables. Although there may have been such a thing as sacred prostitution in other cultures, in India perhaps, there is no reliable evidence in ancient Mesopotamia, Syria-Palestine, or Egypt.[4] Ancient authors such as Herodotus and modern novelists and orientalists even more so were obviously carried away by their erotic fantasies. Temple prostitution belonged to what came "easily to their daydreams packed inside Oriental clichés: harems, princesses, princes, slaves, veils, dancing girls and boys, sherbets, ointments, and so on." The modern as well as the ancient East was associated with licentious sex, untiring sensuality, unlimited desire, and deep generative energies; "the Orient was a place where one could look for sexual experience unobtainable in Europe."[5]

This is not to say, however, that the ancients shared our traditional, Western attitude toward sexuality. It seems that temple prostitution actually existed but without the deep ritual significance with which it was often credited by modern authors. Just as ancient temples owned and cultivated land, were important centers of trade, served as banks, and had their own potters or smiths, they also had prostitutes who offered their services. Although some of these prostitutes may have worshiped a goddess of sexual love, their trade had no ritual meaning.

In Israel, prostitution could be spoken of without disdain. The famous Rahab of Jericho, who appears in the genealogy of Jesus and Tamar, in the book of Genesis, was able to play the harlot without losing face.[6] Prostitutes were outsiders, women who were neither unmarried virgins nor nonvirgin wives. "Once a girl is not seen in the role of daughter, virgin, and nubile woman," explains Susan Niditch, "she is, in effect, outside the rules." For those standing outside the rules, prostitution was a viable trade. "Prostitutes seem to have an accepted, outcast place in Israelite society."[7] Harlotry, then, was a legitimate, although not necessarily desirable and respected, occupation. When King Ahab of Samaria was killed in battle with the Syrians, his blood-stained chariot was washed in the pool of Samaria, while "the dogs licked up his blood, and the harlots washed themselves in it [1 Kings 22:38, RSV]." Dogs and harlots—no doubt this juxtaposition expresses contempt. When in a heated argument the prophet Amos says to a priest, "Your wife shall be a harlot in the city," we get another glimpse of how degrading it must have been for an upper-class woman to become a city prostitute.[8] She

98

would be transferred from the top to the bottom of the social ladder. Although the Jerusalem temple had its brothel for a long time, eventually, in King Josiah's reform (622 B.C.), prostitution was banned from the temple.[9] It was then that the profession was, at least officially, abolished and forbidden. "There shall be no prostitute of the daughters of Israel," proscribes the law, "neither shall there be a cult prostitute of the sons of Israel. You shall not bring the hire of a harlot, or the wages of a dog [male prostitute], into the house of [Yahweh] your God [Deut. 23:17–18]." The injunction about the money was probably addressed to the temple management rather than to the former patrons of the available boys and girls.

Banned from the temple does not mean banned from the street and the tavern. It was there that biblical authors met prostitutes. Tamar, dressed as a harlot, sat at the "entrance" of Enaim, and Rahab's house at the city wall of Jericho seems to have been an inn whose female keeper was a prostitute.[10] That inns served as brothels was also common in ancient Mesopotamia and Greece.[11] As late as A.D. 787 a synod of Nicaea issued a decree forbidding traveling monks and priests to stay at public inns, since these were notoriously frequented by harlots and female musicians.[12] An Akkadian text tells us that harlots are likely to be found sitting "at the entrance of the tavern,"[13] a striking parallel to Lady Folly sitting at the door of her house. The Roman comedian Plautus calls the harlots *prosedae*, girls "sitting in front" of the brothel.[14]

Other places to look for prostitutes were the streets and public squares. "Take a harp, go about the city, O forgotten harlot! Make sweet melody, sing many songs, that you may be remembered [Isa. 23:16, RSV],"[15] is a line from a popular song about an old and visibly worn-out harlot, quoted by prophet Isaiah. A somewhat enigmatic passage, in which Ezekiel compares Israel with a harlot, says that "you built yourself a *gab* in every square and make yourself a *ramah*. At every crossing you built your *ramah* . . . and spread your legs for every passer-by [Ezek. 16:24–25]."[16] The "vaulted chamber" of the *Revised Standard Version* for *gab*, and "lofty place" for *ramah* do not really make sense. The Septuagint is probably correct in translating *gab* as brothel *(oikema pornikon)*, and *ramah*[17] may simply mean house or

99

**Figure 8. Relatives of Folly: dancing harlots
of nineteenth-century Egypt.**

residence. The kind of building required by the context is a tent
or a similar impermanent structure that could easily be erected
in a public square and used for the harlot's trade.

LADY FOLLY

In creating Lady Folly as a figure of fiction, the poet blends
image and reality. For the student, a harlot may be a real danger,
but she also serves as an image for the host of dangers that may
detract him from learning his lesson and lure him from the right
path. The scenario of a student being invited by Wisdom and a
harlot at the same time can be found in the literature of classical
Greece as the myth of Hercules at the Crossroads. Hercules, the
favorite hero of Greek mythology, represents the young man
who, reaching adulthood, must choose between virtue and vice.

100

These two figures are personified as Lady Aretē (Virtue) and Lady Kakia (Vice). When Hercules had almost grown up, he went into solitude to consider whether he should direct his life toward the way of virtue or toward that of vice. While he pondered the problem, there appeared before him two women—one beautiful and virtuous, the other opulent and adorned. Both addressed him, offering their services as guides through life. "Hercules, I see that you are in doubt which path to take toward life," said Lady Vice:

> Make me your friend; follow me, and I will lead you along the pleasantest and easiest road. You shall taste all the sweets of life; and hardship you shall never know. First, of wars and worries you shall not think, but shall ever be considering what choice food or drink you can find.[18]

We can only speculate whether there is any historical connection between Proverbs 9 and the Greek myth, generally traced back to sophist Prodikos of the fifth century B.C. Prodikos may have heard an oriental tale, which he presented in the garb of Greek mythology. Both traditions have in common that vice or folly is represented as a harlot or hetaera. As a poetic figure she represents a man's "bad company." In the didactic discourses of Proverbs 1—7, the adulteress or loose woman serves the same purpose.[19] The seductive woman of a text found in Qumran and the medieval image of "Lady World" are all in the same category.[20] For an exclusively male group, the adulteress and harlot are suitable figures for depicting an enticing but ultimately destructive reality.[21]

CHAPTER 14

Brief Commentary on Proverbs 9:1–6, 11–18

The skillfully crafted poem is in two parts: first, Wisdom invites the listeners to her banquet, or to her school; then, it is Folly's turn to entice the same addressees and lure them into her house. The chances given to the two rivals are unequal. Wisdom is given slightly more space (eight couplets) than is Folly (six couplets), and the latter's invitation is disqualified not only by the name given to the seducing harlot, Folly, but also by the concluding comment that her guests are in the realm of the dead. Wisdom's guests, however, are promised a long and successful life.

It is easy to extract the didactic elements from Wisdom's invitation. Doing this yields the following text:

> 3 *She [Lady Wisdom] calls[1]*
> *From the walls of the city:[2]*
> 4 *"Whoever is immature, let him enter here!"*
> *To him who is without learning[3] she says,*
> 6 *"Get away from the immature, and live!*
> *Get on the way of understanding!*
> 11 *For through me your days will increase,*
> *Your [happy] years will be many.*
> 12 *If you are wise, you are wise for your own [benefit];*
> *If you are a mischief-maker—you bear[4] it alone."*

Wisdom—or perhaps her maid—uses the city wall as a speaker's platform in order to address young people and invite them to enter school or attend class. The setting of the other two poems being repeated,[5] the reader is already familiar with Wisdom's propaganda at the busiest part of the city.

The invitation to attend school comes in the form of a request to leave one's ignorant companions and walk in the "way of understanding." Here we clearly hear the voice of a teacher asking young people to gather around him for instruction. Although the teacher may wish to gather students *on the street* to form a kind of ad hoc class, he may also be calling them into a schoolroom. The actual context of the poem, with the reference to Wisdom's newly built house, seems to suggest the existence of a school building or a sheltered area for a class to assemble and receive tuition.

We can recognize the teacher by the language he speaks. The "way of understanding," like the "way of wisdom,"[6] refers to the ethical content of the instruction. Students will be taught how to live wisely and to be successful. Instruction shows them an alternative, more profitable way of living, a way that should be preferred to the way of ignorance. The term denoting success is *ḥayyim*, commonly translated as "life"; here it refers to life in the fullest possible sense of the term as it often does: a successful, happy, and long life.[7] The didactic language also includes terms used by the teacher to address his young audience. He uses *peti* and *ḥasar-leb*. The *peti* is a young, untutored person who needs to be instructed and set on the right path.[8] The other term, *ḥasar-leb*, literally means someone whose heart (i.e., his mind) is deficient or poor. Here the term is practically synonymous with *peti*, denoting a person, therefore, who is without knowledge and learning and needs to be instructed and guided.[9] The teacher's task is to alleviate this lack of learning; he offers his guidance and endeavors to make the unlearned wise.

The didactic tone of the concluding appeal cannot be overlooked. The lesson taught is not useless and without meaning in life; it is for the student's own benefit. Whoever, as a mischief-maker and ne'er-do-well, is unwilling to learn will remain a fool and will have to bear the consequences.

Wisdom, however, is not only the teacher she represents in Proverbs 1 and in the lines quoted. She is also the goddess of

103

Proverbs 8. The mythical aspects of our poem may be tentatively isolated as follows:

> 1 *When [Lady] Wisdom had built a[10] house,*
> *Had hewn[11] seven pillars,*
> 2 *She slaughtered, spiced the wine,*
> *And[12] set the table.*
> 3 *She sent out the maids to call,*
> 5 *"Come, eat my food,*
> *And drink the wine I have spiced!"*

This is an invitation to the solemn inauguration of a newly erected house. The Talmud rightly observes that Wisdom acts like a king who has built and decorated a palace, prepared a meal, and now asks his guests to come in.[13] The guests are invited by messengers, as is the custom.[14] It is considered problematic by some commentators that this is done by women. Not that Wisdom is not allowed to have maids like any other woman of rank.[15] But it would be against "the Semitic sense of propriety," explains Dahood, for "female servants to invite male guests."[16] One commentator[17] has tried to defend the biblical text by quoting an eighteenth-century Swedish traveler who has witnessed how, in Egypt, singing women moved through the village streets, inviting everyone to a public feast. These women, of course, were accompanied by men. Because eighteenth-century Egyptian village customs are hardly a reliable guide to biblical Israel, we should simply dismiss Dahood's argument. A much better guide is a Hittite myth in which goddess Ashertu sends out her maids to the storm god, inviting him in no ambiguous language: "Come, sleep with me!"[18] Sending out maids to invite male guests may not have been considered improper at all.

Ancient invitations regularly include specific references to what is being served. "Behold, I have made ready my dinner, my oxen and my fat calves are killed, and everything is ready; come to the marriage feast," reads an invitation in the New Testament.[19] Meat and wine were the most common as well as the most valued items advertised to the invited and offered to guests. The feast is built around meat and wine, quite as in the Homeric tradition. Fruits and vegetables, however much they were eaten in daily life, play no role at the festive board.[20] Because it was customary to mix wine with water before drinking it, commentators normally take verse 5b as referring to that custom. But apparently it was also common to spice wine with honey, herbs, and resin, especially on festive occasions. "Whereas the Greeks and Latins by *mixed wine* always understood wine diluted and lowered with water," explains Bishop Lowth,

> the Hebrews, on the contrary, generally mean by it wine made stronger and more inebriating by the addition of higher and more powerful ingredients, such as honey, spices, defrutum (or wine inspissated by boiling it down to two thirds or one half of the quantity), myrrh, mandragora, opiates, and other drugs.[21]

Mixed wine, therefore, is strong, spiced wine. Rather than referring to the everyday custom of mingling wine with water, it seems likely that the poet had in mind the more noteworthy custom of spicing wine.

In order to understand the urgent nature of Wisdom's invitation we have to place it into the context of biblical and Eastern custom. An oriental invitation has two phases; there is a general invitation that is then followed by the summons to come and enter the host's house when everything has actually been prepared. Canon Tristram, a nineteenth-century traveler, explains the procedures involved:

> The intended guests having been apprized some days before of the coming feast, servants are again sent, on the morning of the day, to remind those who have been invited; and the omission of this second summons would be a grievous breach of etiquette, equivalent to a cancelling of the previous more general notification. To refuse the second summons would be an insult which is equivalent among the Arab tribes to a declaration of war.[22]

Wisdom's invitation is in the second phase, when the table is set, the food has been prepared, and the servants are sent out. If hospitality is refused now, it would be a grave insult.

The two elements, mythical imagery and didactic wisdom, remain separate, although they are mixed and juxtaposed in the text. It is up to the reader to make the connection between both

105

parts, to use imagination to decode the poet's message. One is told, with reference to mythical terms, that the school is the Wisdom's banquet. Happy are those who follow the invitation!

Wisdom's antagonist also issues an invitation whose style is didactic as well:

> 16 *Whoever is immature, let him enter here!*

This is verbally identical with Wisdom's invitation of verse 4 and no doubt echoes the way a teacher offers his services. Wisdom and Folly speak the same language. Folly imitates Wisdom, ridiculing her invitation. (Serious words always sound ridiculous and stupid when someone else repeats them in parrot fashion.) More than that, changing an invitation to attend school into an invitation to visit a doubtful tavern or a brothel seems blasphemous. Yet the parody may also have a deeper significance. A harlot introduces an inexperienced person to the seamier side of city life. Relying on her experience, she considers her trade as a special kind of schooling that gives sexual wisdom to inexperienced men. The Babylonian epic of Gilgamesh, for instance, has a harlot appear in this kind of "teaching" role. She is hired to seduce and tame Enkidu, the inexperienced Tarzanlike man of the wilderness, to make him fit for living in the city of Uruk, to which she leads him. The harlot "freed her breasts, bared her bosom," and they copulated for six days and seven nights. After his sexual initiation, Enkidu "had wisdom, broader understanding." "Thou art wise, Enkidu," says the harlot, "art become like a god."[23] Given the education some of the harlots had as musicians, dancers, reciters of love poetry, and the like,[24] it is not surprising that their trade could be credited with a dimension of teaching. Their sensuality itself appears as "learned."

The closing sentence of the poem is pointed and abrupt:

> 18 *Yet he does not know that the Rephaïm are there,*
> *That her guests are in the depth of Sheol.*

The house of the seductress is linked to Sheol (i.e., the nether world of Hebrew mythology) and its foremost denizens, the

Rephaïm or ancestral spirits.[25] The one seduced is unaware of his doom; he walks blindly into the trap.[26] In their warnings of seductive women, be they harlots or adulteresses, the teachers indiscriminately use whatever metaphor of destruction comes to their mind. "Her steps follow the path to Sheol," says one text.[27] Another one calls the harlot "a deep pit,"[28] and elsewhere, as in the text, her house becomes a veritable gateway to the nether world.[29] She leads the simpleton like an ox to the slaughter, or she lures him into her snare like a bird.[30] The images are to give the impression that such a woman will treat her patrons in as hostile and pitiless a fashion as death. Whatever inhibitions and latent fears a young man might have, including the fear of entering an unfamiliar place, the teachers exploit it. They make the harlot look like a monster, and her house, like the gateway to hell. By using images and metaphors the teachers underscore the high price to be paid by those who have dealings with this woman; the price is moral and social death. They do not talk about the ideal student who remains firm and under self-control, turning his back on the harlot. Rather, the teachers seek to impress students with the seriousness of the situation. It is safe to assume that there will be folly and that young men are not necessarily equipped to deal with it. The didactic purpose of the poem is clear enough: Folly causes misfortune, doom, and destruction. So, stay away from the harlot and her house!

Only in the closing couplet of the poem is the perspective of the teacher and moralist betrayed. The rest of the text describes what the harlot does, where she may be found, and how she approaches her prospective patrons:

13   *Lady Folly[31] bustles about.[32]*
       Knowing seduction and nothing else,[33]
14   *She places herself at the entrance of her house,*
       [Using] the city wall as a chair,[34]
15   *In order to call those who pass by*
       Keeping straight their paths.
16   *. . . "enter here," . . . she says,*
17   *"Stolen water is sweet,*
       And bread [gotten] in secret is tasty."

107

Like her famous colleague, Rahab of Jericho, the harlot lives by the city wall.[35] It seems that the city wall was the usual place for taverns, which often served as brothels as well. A passage in the Talmud calls the owner of an inn "him who takes his seat at the city walls," listing him with equally abominable people: people of rank frequenting brothels, men engaging in prostitution, and those who enter their neighbor's bedroom uninvited.[36]

The harlot sits at the door of her house waiting for patrons and talking to the men who happen to pass by. It might have been enough for her just to sit and wait. After all, the house of a harlot at the city wall is well known and may have displayed a scarlet piece of cloth, indicative of her trade.[37] She is "dressed as a harlot," wearing tight clothes to good effect and perhaps granting glimpses of some of her charms.[38] Compared with the clothes of ordinary, modest women, the harlot's dress is sophisticated and provocative. Anyone who sees a fashionable woman sitting alone at the entrance to a city must conclude that she is a harlot.[39] When she spreads her legs in an enticing gesture,[40] there can be no doubt about her trade.

Yet the poet is not satisfied with having the harlot just sit there and wait. He presents her as a woman who is eagerly soliciting patrons, noisily drawing the attention of passing men to her charms. She is intent on seducing men. By saying that she calls "those who pass by, keeping straight their paths," he makes a finely drawn moral point. She tries to draw men away from not only their honest, everyday work, but also the "straight" path of wisdom.[41]

The harlot invites men to share "bread and water." This seems to suggest that, compared with Wisdom, she has not much to offer. Bread and water, offered in a tavern, are poor substitutes for meat and wine, offered at a festive banquet. This reading, however, does not exhaust the subtle invitation. The water is called "stolen," and the bread was gotten "in secret." To the initiate, "drinking stolen water" and eating bread gotten "in secret" refer to sexual intercourse. What we have here is part of the coded language of prostitutes, a language that was no doubt easily understood by whomever the harlot addressed.[42] The Septuagint inserted a few lines that develop the image without altering the sense:

> But hasten away, delay not in the place,
> Neither fix thine eye upon her,
> For thus shalt thou go through alien water;
> But do thou abstain from alien water,
> And drink not of an alien fountain,
> That thou mayest live long, and years of life may be added
> to thee.

The expression "to drink of an alien fountain" is presumably as clear and unmistakable as "drinking stolen water." It is safe to assume that anyone but a child would have understood the hidden reference.

The teacher's concluding note places the student in an observer's position. The seduced one does not know "that her guests are in the depth of Sheol." As an observer, he may see and understand the lesson.

PART FOUR

WHO IS WISDOM?

CHAPTER 15

Mysterious Wisdom

To understand a poem properly one has to be aware of its cultural context. One needs to know something about the fiction and poetry of the time and, as far as possible, about the author and the times in which the author lived. As regards Old Testament scholarship, this kind of research is severely hampered. Only a limited number of poems are available to us; there are no theoretical discussions dealing specifically with poetry; and the authors are always anonymous. Consequently, Old Testament scholarship had to develop its own methodology to suit this situation. The notion of *Sitz im Leben des Volkes* or setting in popular life, that is, the question of the original function of a text studied in the light of a repertoire of motifs, stylistic and formal elements, has turned out to be extremely valuable here. The fact that research occasionally has become totally analytical while neglecting the fundamental unity of the text can be no argument against the basic validity of the approach.

In this final section I am going to explore the still unanswered question of the unity of the poems. Without a prior notion of "Lady Wisdom," the three poems under discussion could never have been written. The "Lady Wisdom" motif establishes the internal unity of each poem and relates them to one another. Yet the figure of Wisdom is a mystery. It is not simply that one is unlikely to meet her in the square or at the city gate, as we might normally expect to meet other people. Wisdom is also an enigma to scholarly research. Although there have been numerous studies of Wisdom, we have no clear conception of her identity and origin.

In the three poems Wisdom appears in more than one role. It has been relatively easy to define her role in Proverbs 1 and Proverbs 9. In the former poem she is a *teacher* standing on the square in front of the city gate gathering students about her. In the latter poem she is a *lady of rank* (or a *goddess* if a fragment of a myth is quoted) who keeps herself more distant. Instead of appearing in public, she sends out her ladies-in-waiting to invite young people to a festive banquet. It is considerably more difficult to determine the role of Wisdom in Proverbs 8. In the first few lines of the poem she appears as a *teacher* gathering students around her (vss. 1–11). Then, she suddenly changes her tone, speaks like a proud *goddess* who puts kings and nobles into office (vss. 12–21) and tells of her origins before the world was made and of her childlike play at the dawn of creation (vss. 22–31). Even her role as an infant-goddess is not the final one. In the end the poem reverts to its original theme, showing Wisdom in the role of a *teacher* (vss. 32–36, with possible undertones of the role of a lover in vs. 35). It is clear why school wisdom should be pictured as a teacher warning, correcting, and urging her students to attend class. Even the poet's use of the image of a woman of rank may be considered an understandable and imaginative use of imagery. But what is the meaning of Wisdom's *divine* attributes?

Scholars confront us with a number of incompatible views: (a) According to some authors, she is derived from a pagan, perhaps Canaanite, goddess of Wisdom, and the poems actually echo an ancient myth. (b) Others bring her close to God. Like the Holy Spirit in later Christian thought, she is a being ultimately indistinguishable from God. A half-independent figure, her function is in revealing the deity itself. (c) Others again consider Wisdom as anything but a goddess or supernatural being. Rather, she is the product of poetic imagination, a poetic personification of human wisdom or even of the somehow divine cosmic order. Any mythological expressions or divine attributes would be powerful poetic devices, skillfully used by someone who does not believe in the existence of gods other than Yahweh, the God of Israel.[1]

114

Although the second suggestion (b) does not seem to recommend itself, the other two sound plausible but contradict each other. Yet can they be reconciled? The poet, it could be argued, embellished his poems not by drawing from scattered mythological sources; instead, he relied on a particular body of ancient Canaanite mythology. He took an ancient Canaanite or early Hebrew goddess of wisdom and her mythology as his guiding and inspiring model. This view assumes a distance from pagan, if not Hebrew, mythology, which is, however, not easily imaginable during the time of the monarchy. Should one place our poems, therefore, in the supposedly safe, orthodox religious climate of the late postexilic period, in which anything polytheistic and pagan had long since ceased to be appealing to the Jewish mind? In a period, therefore, in which the poet could start to "play" with ancient mythology because it had lost its *religious* power over the mind while keeping its *aesthetic* fascination?

On the one hand, it can be argued that, in composing his texts, the poet did not feel so distant toward pagan mythology. Like many other Israelites, he could in fact actually have believed that there are many gods and goddesses besides Yahweh, and that Wisdom was one of them. As a contemporary of the Hebrew monarchy, the author would either not have respected the injunction not to recognize other gods besides Yahweh or not have been familiar with it. For him, Wisdom was as legitimate a goddess as any other deity he and many of his contemporaries worshiped.

By saying this I am not suggesting that it is impossible to offer a reasonable interpretation of the evidence, even if it is a guess. I am, however, insisting that an interpretation only makes sense in the context of a comprehensive reconstruction of ancient Israelite religious history or, more specifically, a plausible view of the origins and development of monotheism.

CHAPTER 16

The Origin and Nature of Biblical Monotheism

Biblical scholars usually agree that monotheism, or something very much like monotheism, started in the time of King Josiah rather than in the time of Abraham or Moses.[1] In 622 B.C. a scroll was brought to the Judean king Josiah (641–609) and read out to him. The book, allegedly discovered during the restoration of the Jerusalem temple, contained a code of law that no one until then had followed and that overthrew all previous ritual practice. It demanded the abolition of the cults of all divinities other than Yahweh, who was the only one who might be worshiped in the temple at Jerusalem. The high priest Hilkiah, high-ranking officials, and a prophetess consulted on the matter supported the book, and Josiah made it the law of the state.

Judah now had a written codification of its religion, of a kind known in comparative religion as "monolatrous." Perhaps other gods and goddesses existed, but Judah was to worship only its national God, Yahweh. Even if the king's reform was less stringent than the biblical narrative reports, it nevertheless gives a good idea of Israel's traditional *polytheistic* religion. "And he deposed the idolatrous priests . . . who burned incense to Baal, to the sun, and the moon, and the constellations, and all the host of the heavens."[2]

116

It is generally accepted today that the reforming code of law constitutes the basis of the book of Deuteronomy. It is more difficult to determine the age and origin of the retrieved text. Perhaps the find was only a pious fraud, and the ink on the scroll was scarcely dry when it was read to the king.

But the Yahweh-alone movement behind the book was no new thing. Luckily, there is a historical work indebted to the Deuteronomic body of thought that enables us to reconstruct the movement's image of its own history. The Yahweh-alone movement saw itself as beginning in the mists of prehistory, in the legendary time of Moses. Yahweh had revealed himself to Moses and had given him his law. Although it is impossible to determine when Moses and his successor Joshua lived, we can discern a sequence of more or less distinctly historical events:

1. In the ninth-century northern kingdom of Israel there was a fierce confrontation between a Yahweh-alone movement and worshipers of a god called Baal. King Ahab (874–853) supported Baal worship, but the prophet Elijah opposed it. King Jehoram (852–834) restricted it, and Jehu (841–813) finally got rid of Baal worship altogether.

2. In the eighth century, Hosea, a prophet active in the northern kingdom, became a strong advocate of the exclusive worship of Yahweh. It is true that Hosea is not mentioned in the Deuteronomic history, but the spirit and langauge of Deuteronomy itself are clearly indebted to him.

3. In the southern kingdom King Hezekiah of Judah (728–699) introduced a cultic reform that satisfied major demands of the Yahweh-alone movement. He destroyed the places where other gods were worshiped, broke up idols, and cleansed the Jerusalem temple of pagan accretions.

Biblical criticism has expended a great deal of ingenuity on establishing a prehistory to Josiah's reform. Unfortunately, the results are only provisional and still contested by researchers. Moses, taken to be a historical figure, is probably to be located in the thirteenth century B.C. He may possibly have introduced the worship of Yahweh. But the Yahweh-alone idea seems to be alien to him. Many people have heard of Sigmund Freud's psychoanalytical midrash *Moses and Monotheism* (1939). Freud claimed to detect in the religion of Yahweh an echo of the fourteenth-century Egyptian belief in Aton. Admittedly, Psalm 104 must be indebted to religious verse of the Egyptian Amarna period, but Freud's thesis has been abandoned as outdated. The study is still valuable as an analysis of the religious father figure, but it is invalid as a contribution to the history of monotheism. The figure of Moses and his ideas are still obscured by the usual shadows cast over religious origins. Joshua's covenant discourse at a tribal assembly at Shechem is just as much a product of pious fantasy as the nighttime destruction of a pagan temple related in the book of Judges.[3] Moses' successors, including Joshua and the judges, remain in the shadowland of legend and have not yet emerged into the light of real history.

Unfortunately, ninth-century events are almost as obscure. King Ahab's wife, Jezebel, a princess from the Phoenician city of Sidon, seems to have introduced alien cults. Why and by whom these were resisted we do not know. Perhaps the new temples attracted a vast number of people so that the old places of worship lost out financially. Economic envy can occur in the religious world too. We have no idea what course the conflict ran. The most certain fact is the removal of a cultic symbol dedicated to Baal from the Samarian capital. King Joram (852–841) is said to have been responsible for its removal. In 841 Jehu usurped his throne. King Jehu had Jezebel (by now Ahab's widow) murdered and killed the Baal worshipers. This perhaps indicates his withdrawal from a foreign policy oriented toward Sidon and Tyre. Jehu was more interested in Assyria. A stela in the British Museum shows Jehu kneeling before the Assyrian monarch Shalmaneser and paying tribute to him.[4] With Jezebel's death the close connection with Phoenicia came to an end; perhaps the Assyrians had already been implicated in Jehu's usurpation. According to the biblical account, the cult of Baal was rejected because worship of Yahweh alone was the ideal. But the existence of any such idea in the ninth century is improbable.

In the book of the prophet Hosea, who lived around 750 B.C. in the northern kingdom, we find the first clear statement of a requirement to worship Yahweh alone: "I am [Yahweh] your God from the land of Egypt; you know no God but me, and besides me there is no savior [Hos. 13:4, RSV]." What a Jew or Christian would take as a reference to the decalogue is rather the

118

basis of the much later ten commandments, which in their turn depend on the statement in Hosea. Clearly, only a small group advocated Yahwistic monolatry in the time of Hosea. The official temple religion was not interested in the novelty: "They kept sacrificing to the Baals and burning incense to idols [Hos. 11:2, RSV]." On several occasions it is obvious that worship of Yahweh alone is an extension and intensification of the struggle against Baal from the previous century. The "other gods" are merely called "the Baals." "And I will punish her for the feast days of the Baals when she burned incense to them," is one Hosean assertion; another says: "I will remove the names of the Baals from her [Israel's] mouth [Hos. 2:13, 17, RSV]." The opposition was no longer merely to the Baal of Sidon, but to *all* local manifestations of Baal. Wherever Baal was worshiped, the Yahweh-alone movement rejected the cult. The same was true of other gods who did not belong to the Baal type of deity—the plague god, the death god, the love goddess, and so on. The explicit reference to *the Baals* is probably due not so much to the popularity of Baal shrines, but much more to the memory of the "original conflict" in the ninth century between supporters of Yahweh and those of Sidonian Baal. Accordingly, all gods are denounced as "Baals"—as (alleged) competitors of Yahweh.

Under King Hezekiah of Judah one finds the first trace in the southern kingdom of the influence of the Yahweh-alone idea. After the political disappearance of the northern kingdom (722), a few people who belonged to the movement may have come to Jerusalem and soon found supporters there. Hezekiah is credited with an ambitious cultic reform that must have been, in reality, rather modest.[5]

The king had a sacred tree (Hebr. *'asherah*) and a bronze serpent removed from the temple. That produced an aniconic cult of Yahweh in the temple. The reason for the reform is not known. Perhaps the measure was taken under pressure from the aloneist movement during the Assyrian military invasion, when there was reason to fear that the southern kingdom would fall as the northern one had. In that case more protection would have been expected from the Yahweh of aniconic worship than from a god whose power was represented by cultic symbols. Obviously, iconoclasm was now part of the program of the Yahweh-alone movement, and people began to follow it, although perhaps only in times of need.

THE BREAKTHROUGH TO MONOTHEISM

With the death (or murder?) of Josiah in 609, the last outstanding period of the Jewish monarchy came to an end. Once again, sacrifice was offered to "Baal, to the sun, and the moon, and the constellations, and all the host of the heavens [2 Kings 23:5, RSV]." The Yahweh-alone movement, however, had taken such firm hold that it was no longer possible to suppress it. In the last years of the monarchy it found eloquent spokesmen in the prophets Jeremiah and Ezekiel. Both came from priestly families, were grounded in the aloneist movement of the time of Josiah, and carried the monolatrous idea into the Babylonian exile. In Jeremiah one can observe an important development of the divine image. The prophet sees Yahweh as the creator of the world: "It is I who by my great power and my outstretched arm have made the earth, . . . and I give it to whomever it seems right to me [Jer. 27:5, RSV]."[6] This statement of 594 B.C. depicts Yahweh in the image of the Babylonian creator-god Marduk. At the same time the God of Israel bestows the overlordship of the world on the Babylonian king Nebuchadnezzar. Yahweh has been elevated to the rank of Creator, with dominion over the world, and is already almost the universal God of monotheism.

One generation after Jeremiah the anonymous prophet called Deutero-Isaiah completed the concept. The benevolent rule of the Persians having replaced Babylonian imperialism, Deutero-Isaiah acknowledges the Persian king Cyrus as the "messiah" appointed by Yahweh. And he is the first to see Yahweh as *the one and only God* besides whom there are no other gods. An encounter with the old monotheistic religion of Zoroaster, which was widespread among the Persians, would seem to have given the prophet this idea. The Jews living in the Persian empire discovered a related faith in the Zoroastrian religion that won considerable respect among them. Indeed, in their own tradition the Jews now found several related teachings and customs and thereafter stressed them specially: the doctrine of creation, the uniqueness of God, and the significance of purity and die-

120

tary laws. Even in the sixth century there were sporadic Jewish echoes of the Zoroastrian doctrines of the next world and the resurrection.[7] In this case they were even prepared to adopt new teachings from the cognate religion; these, however, took hold only centuries later.

Under the influence of Deutero-Isaiah, monotheism also entered Deuteronomy and the Deuteronomic history. Monotheistic statements were inserted when these writings took final shape— see Deuteronomy 4:35: "Yahweh is God, there is no other besides him." The revision was consciously made the last possible one; henceforth "you shall not add to it or take from it [Deut. 12:32, RSV]." Not even prophets were allowed to propose any new doctrines.

The monotheistic profession of faith became the yardstick for the formation of the biblical canon. It could adopt only what was compatible with the Yahweh-alone idea or its advanced form, monotheism. Everything else was transformed in the process of revision or thrown out. The Old Testament canon, therefore, contains only a few testimonies to the old polytheistic belief once shared by almost all Israelites.

With Deutero-Isaiah and the Deuteronomic literature of the sixth (and possibly fifth) century, we reach the end of a development that had begun some three hundred years before. Judaism now possessed its monotheistic creed, which it bore unaltered through the course of history, to be handed on to Christianity and Islam. Monotheism is the gift to humankind of the biblical religion.

After this attempt to sketch the evolution, or perhaps revolution, of monotheism, it is time to look into its principles. How was it that the state deity of a small, politically and culturally insignificant nation reached the status of the universal God?

FROM STATE GOD TO THE UNIVERSAL GOD OF MONOTHEISM

Polytheistic religions are also acquainted with the idea of the worship of one particular god and no other. Hence the position of Yahweh as Israel's national god was uncontested. All the surrounding nations had *one* god for the country and nation—

121

the Moabites worshiped Chemosh; the Ammonites, Milcom; the Assyrians, Ashur; and the Egyptians, Amun-Re. The prophet Micah sums up the principle of the national deity thus: "All the peoples walk each in the name of its god, but we will walk in the name of [Yahweh] our God for ever and ever [Mic. 4:5, RSV]." These national gods are especially concerned with war and peace, military supremacy, the well-being of monarchs, and so forth. In polytheistic Israel, however, other gods and goddesses were worshiped: deities who were responsible for female fertility, family health and prosperity, wind and weather, and so on; each deity, therefore, had his or her allotted area of responsibility.

Nevertheless, the particular position of certain individuals made them interested in the worship only of Yahweh. This did not mean that they enjoyed an exclusive relationship with this god, let alone demanded that of others. Included among these people was the Davidic royal house, which had a special relationship with Yahweh and indeed had built a temple for him in the immediate vicinity of the Jerusalem palace. Among them, above all, were the prophets of Yahweh: for a man (or a woman) called by Yahweh to be his spokesman and messenger could have no great interest in other gods. No prophet can serve two masters simultaneously—for instance, Yahweh and Baal. For the same reason it was easy for the Yahweh-alone movement to arrogate the books of Yahweh prophets to itself or even rework them in its own favor. Amos and Isaiah were prophets of Yahweh: that is, they prophesied only in the name of Yahweh. They offered no messages from other gods. Although they themselves honored only Yahweh—"[Yahweh] alone will be exalted [Isa. 2:11, RSV]"—they showed no sign of demanding worship of Yahweh alone. Probably the most appropriate description of their faith is "polytheistic."

One reason it is easy to pick Yahweh out of the many gods worshiped in Palestine is that Yahweh is distinctive in having no relatives in the mythical world of the gods. He is neither the son of another god, nor has he any wife or descendants.[8] What exactly does that mean?

Every god has characteristics and a history narrated about him. The fact that Yahweh cannot only become the opponent of other gods, but also the opponent of *all* divinities must lie in his nature as unfolded and explained in myth. Eastern mythology, however, usually tells not merely of one god alone, but of several deities who are associated in various ways. The usual form of connection is marriage, family, and kinship. Like ourselves, the gods do not appear as isolated individuals, but are encountered within a network of kinship. The Egyptian Isis is Osiris' wife and Horus' mother—to name only one example. Apart from this genealogical form of organization, mythology also features the divine state with a king, parliamentary body, and hierarchy, especially among the Sumerians. The Old Testament also acknowledges the notion of a heavenly court, but this is incidental.[9] Yahweh appears as the outsider and loner who stands apart from the usual associations. Yahweh is a childless and unmarried god.

Researchers into pre-Islamic religion have constantly reported the existence of childless gods: they are described as *'abtar,* which means "without a son."[10] As a lonely god of this kind, Yahweh has little to do with the highly structured world of Canaanite deities. Whoever worships Yahweh does not have to honor the entire range of divinities at one and the same time, for Yahweh is related to none of them.[11] His claim to power will not make anyone his rival. No cousin will wax great in his shadow; no son will involve him in a conflict of the generations and take his place in the end. In societies with kin forms of organization, special claims by individuals are usually treated by relations with little or no respect. The saying that a prophet is not honored in his own country and in his own house[12] indicates the egalitarian ideal of kin groups. As a solitary god, Yahweh did not have to accord with such an ideal and could all the more readily reach the status of the only God.

This elevation was made possible by the "temporary monolatry" of oriental gods.[13] A scene from the Akkadian Atrahasis epic will illustrate the nature of this institution. When a plague breaks out in the country it is attributed to the anger of the plague god, Namtara. Therefore, they decide to sacrifice only to Namtara for a time and to neglect all other gods. This preferential treatment is enough to make the plague god change his mind. Because he is appeased he stops the plague. At another

123

point in the same epic the same treatment is given to Adad, the rain god, who restores his rain after a period of drought. If a deity is accorded the special honor of "provisional monolatry," then he or she has to accede to human wishes and help the worshipers in their great need.

There are three clear examples of temporary monolatry in the Bible:

> —Jeremiah 44:18: This text presupposes that only Yahweh was worshiped during the siege of Jerusalem and that the cults of other deities were suspended.
>
> —Daniel 6:8: The Persian king demands exclusive worship of himself, lasting thirty days.
>
> —Daniel 11:37–38: Here we are told of a king who orders all the gods to be neglected with the exception of a certain "god of fortresses"; doubtless a war god is intended.

It is worth noting that temporary monolatry was also known among, and often practiced by, pre-Islamic Arabs. It was accorded the highest God of all, Allah. Mohammed repeatedly complained about this custom, for as soon as the petitioner was freed from his distress, he ended his exclusive worship of Allah (see, for instance, Sura 31:31–32, which mentions distress at sea and being brought safe to land). This was tantamount to a temporary orthodoxy, which could only make the prophet angry.

If we look at the history of the Yahweh-alone movement in connection with the political history of Israel, the notion of temporary monolatry can be offered as an explanation. We have to consider the distribution of political power. From the ninth century onward the two petty kingdoms of Israel and Judah increasingly entered the sphere of influence of the Near Eastern powers. Both countries became subject to tribute and dependent on Assyria. In 722 the northern kingdom was downgraded to an Assyrian province, and after 586 the southern kingdom also became an administrative district. During the continuously critical period between the two dates a group made itself known that I have called the Yahweh-alone movement. It demanded the exclusive worship of the national deity. Only he who was concerned with the well-being of the state could be expected to help. When Judah as a state was crushed by the power of Babylon, the idea arose of a one and only God who ruled the whole world. Accordingly, monotheism is a reaction to a political crisis, one in which no further aid can be expected of diplomacy and foreign military. There is only one savior: the one God. The history of the rise of monotheism is part of a broader history: that of the destruction of a small state.

Clearly, monotheism as a doctrine could not solve Israel's political problems. But even when the doctrinal aspect of monotheism is stressed, Yahweh-alone supporters and early Jewish monotheists were not interested in dogma. That only developed with the fathers of the church and the scholastic theologians with their primarily speculative concerns. The theology of the Yahweh-alone movement is a theology of hope, one that wagers everything on *one* person, on Yahweh. Everything is hoped of him. Hosea and Second Isaiah emphasize it: there is no God other than Yahweh *who will act as a savior.*[14]

In theological jargon one might put it thus: Soteriological monotheism is older and more fundamental than dogmatic belief in one God. Or, hope is older and more basic than belief.

CHAPTER 17

Wisdom: A Hebrew Goddess Redefined

How does monolatric, if not monotheistic, Judaism cope with its polytheistic past? In the Deuteronomic history the official polytheism of the nation is unsparingly stigmatized. Perhaps the "reform kings," Hezekiah and Josiah, were transfigured into national heroes, but otherwise, there is no inclination to gloss over the faults of any member of the royal dynasty. The Deuteronomist's denunciations are even surpassed by Ezekiel, whose chapter 20 finds nothing positive or even edifying in Israel's past. Explains Koch:

> It is hard to find any document in the literature of the world which presents the history of its own people so unfavourably, as a history of guilt. Israel is described as an assembly of human beings who from the very beginnings foolishly and obstinately reject their own salvation. It is a people which never obeys the wise and intelligible laws of its God, and which has behaved worse than all the other nations on earth.[1]

Given this attitude toward the past, it is clear that the canon of sacred literature that emerged gradually after the exile does not contain anything of the polytheistic literature that must have existed. It is completely lost. Defamation of the fathers and the outlawing of their literary heritage, however, are not the only methods of dealing with the past. Besides these relatively unsophisticated methods there are more subtle ones: assimilating, adopting, and reinterpreting traditions that may conserve polytheistic elements within a monotheistic context.

The divine name of Shaddai provides an example of this. Just as the Babylonian called his protecting spirit *shedu,* which is a kind of guardian angel whom he considers to be a minor but accessible deity, so the Israelite polytheist acknowledged his Shaddai. Yahweh-aloneists identified Shaddai with Yahweh, who thus acquired the new role of the individual's protecting spirit to supplement his status as the national deity. This identification, however, did not imply that the name and notion of Shaddai were forgotten and no longer used. In the book of Job, a monotheistic document dating from the fifth century,[2] Yahweh, in his role as personal god, is actually called Shaddai. Klaus Koch who studied this curious phenomenon concludes his analysis as follows:

> The deity, not polymorphous but manifold, approaches man in various extensions, refractions or modes, however one may call this concept. The poet's monotheism is not monolithic. Shaddai is one of these specific refractions, one aspect of God which relates to the human individual, comes close to his body to make him either happy or to wound him deeply. The Shaddai of the Job dialogue is not the Almighty One as some of the modern translations have it, but rather the divine neighbor, somehow to be compared to the personal guardian angel of later centuries.[3]

As Shaddai, Yahweh is particularly responsible for the individual and the well-being of his family. Just compare how happy Job was "while Shaddai was still there at my side, and my servants stood round me, while my path flowed with milk, and the rocks streamed oil."[4]

The name of Shaddai conserved its own message for a long time after the abolition of its originally polytheistic meaning. This can be seen from a Jewish custom based on Deuteronomy 6:9 that is still alive and practiced today. This commandment tells us of the Deuteronomic creed formulas to "write them up on the doorposts of your houses and on your gates." The commandment is fulfilled by writing the text of Deuteronomy 6:4 and some parallel passages on a slip of parchment, the reverse of

Figure 9. A relative of Wisdom: Seshat, Egyptian goddess of writing.

which is inscribed with "Shaddai." The rolled-up parchment is enclosed in a little case, and through a small opening one can read the name of Shaddai. This amulet, called *mezuzah*, is attached to the doorpost to ensure the blessing of God or, to use the older and more original name, Shaddai. A rendering of this name would be "my god," which is, in fact, occasionally used by the Septuagint.[5]

Beautiful polytheistic texts about an Israelite goddess can be found in Proverbs, chapters 1—9. The goddess is called *hokmah*—in English, Wisdom or Shrewdness—and was only later taken to be a simple poetic personification of school wisdom or of God's own wisdom. But to take Proverbs 8:22–30 as referring to the wisdom of the only God is contrary to sound textual analysis, as was observed by the Hispano-Arabic Muslim polemicist Ibn Ḥazm in the eleventh century.[6] And he is right, for Wisdom is the goddess of school and instruction or, more precisely, the divine patroness of scribal education and training. Elsewhere in the ancient East scribes also had their female patron deity. The Sumerians called her *Nisaba*, giving her the beautiful title of "Mistress of Science," while the Egyptians referred to *Seshat* as "she who directs the house of books."[7]

At least according to their teachers, the students are expected to entertain an especially intimate and personal relationship with the school goddess. Proverbs 8:17 alludes to the loving relationship when the goddess says, "Those who love me I love." Proverbs 7:4 is even more explicit: a text inviting the student to declare his love to her. He is to say, "You are my sister," which in plain English is something like, "You are my darling (or sweetheart)." (For the Hebrew, "sister" was a pet name for a female friend or wife.) A further example of erotic language is Proverbs 4:5–9, where the sequence of "acquiring" and "embracing" is unambiguous. The student is not just to have an affair with this goddess, but a permanent marital relationship.

Mythologically, Wisdom's father is the creator god who is called Yahweh. As suggested in the present study, Yahweh may be nothing other than a postexilic, orthodox substitute for the original El who was the actual creator deity of Syro-Palestinian mythology.

As argued in Chapter 16, a national god such as Yahweh need not be conceived of as the creator of humankind or the universe. For most ancient Israelites, as well as for their immediate neighbors, men and women and the world were created by a mighty god called El or Elohim. Accordingly, one biblical text speaks of "El the Most High, creator of heaven and earth."[8] At least one passage gives clear evidence of a later and quite conscious identification of Elohim with Yahweh, thus supplanting earlier views. "Elohim [i.e., Yahweh] formed man from the dust of the ground," reads Genesis 2:7 from the well-known account of creation. The addition of the name Yahweh betrays how the earlier concept of Elohim was supplanted by the belief in Yahweh alone. By adding the name of Yahweh to that of Elohim, an aloneist editor claimed polytheistic mythology for the aloneist faith.

Apart from passages dealing with Wisdom, there is at least one further hint concerning the original polytheistic nature of Proverbs 1—9. It is in the closing line of this self-contained little manual: "The beginning of wisdom is the fear of Yahweh, and knowledge of the holy one(s) is understanding [Prov. 9:10]."[9] I have argued that the original text probably read, "The beginning of wisdom is the fear of *the gods,* and knowledge of the holy ones is understanding." Substituting *'elohim,* gods, for Yahweh, one gets a perfectly balanced couplet. The gods and the holy ones were the deities of polytheistic Israel, among whom Wisdom belonged.

Perhaps the school goddess was a rather pale figure of which the students were not particularly fond, despite her erotic appeal. It was all too evident that the schoolmasters were putting their own exhortations into her divine mouth. Hence she cannot be dangerous to Yahweh-alone or monotheistic doctrine, and reduced to a mere figure of poetic speech, she leads a miserable life in the textbook of postexilic apprentice scribes. There is the possibility, however, that her original nature was remembered in certain polytheistic (i.e., nonconverted) Jewish circles. During the years 1906 to 1908, while working on the Nile island of Elephantine, German archaeologists discovered a bundle of papyrus leaves that turned out to be an Aramaic version of the well-known Assyrian Ahiqar story. The leaves date from the fifth century B.C. and were read by members of the Jewish military colony. Other sources indicate that they worshiped Yahweh along with other gods and goddesses. They were polytheists. One passage of the Ahiqar story, first reconstructed by Arthur Ungnad from two papyrus pages, refers to a goddess who bears exactly the same name as Israel's divine patroness of wisdom.[10] Like the Ahiqar story as a whole, the home of this goddess called Wisdom must be seventh-century Mesopotamia or perhaps Syria. Unfortunately, the Ahiqar passage on Wisdom is too brief and fragmentary to allow for further conclusions. Israel's school goddess may have had innumerable relatives in Near Eastern mythology. What is especially interesting, however, is the identical name, Wisdom. Perhaps the Aramaic-speaking scribes shared the cult of Wisdom with their Hebrew-speaking colleagues.

A polytheistic reading of the poems on Wisdom may help us to understand their original meaning but certainly misses the intention of the editors who received the book of Proverbs into the biblical canon. As committed monotheists, they demythologized Wisdom. In the process of demythologizing, a vital (or perhaps not-so-vital) goddess degenerated into a mere poetic being of ornamental value. Without altogether abandoning the polytheistic rhetoric, the aloneists "sterilized" the ideology from which the poems were derived. The old vocabulary survived—in the form of cut flowers that are beautiful but without life.

For the monotheist reader, Wisdom lost much of her original reality and vitality. What remained was a shadowy figure with some poetic charm. The orthodox reader had to be satisfied with this. A nostalgic memory of the pagan gods is possible and permissible, not for a Jew, but for a Friedrich Schiller:

> *The meadows mourn for the old hollowing life;*
> *Vainly we search the earth of gods bereft;*
> *Where once the warm and living shapes were rife*
> *Shadows alone are left![11]*

What Schiller says of Greek mythology also applies to polytheistic survivals in Judaism. Shadows alone are left!

PERSONIFICATION: POETIC AND MYTHOLOGICAL

In the language of literary criticism and in the jargon of religious studies there is a category appropriate to define the nature of Wisdom: she is a *personification*. This term has occasionally been applied to Wisdom, but rarely have scholars endeavored to define what they mean by the term.[12]

Pötscher proposes to distinguish between poetic personifications and those that belong to what he calls the "realm-as-personality" complex.[13] His example of a playful *poetic personification* is Good Conscience appearing as a female figure on the stage of baroque theater. Although no one believes in the existence of a transcendent character called Good Conscience, everyone enjoys listening to what she has to say. By treating as a person what is not strictly personal, the poet or dramatist adds to the charm of the presentation. Pöscher's examples of *mythological personifications* are Heaven and Earth as deities in ancient Greek religion. Such deities are of a wide variety; while some are endowed with a quite distinctive character, others are rather pale and thus close to poetic figures of speech. The general rule on which the "realm-as-personality" complex is based is well expressed by Cicero: "Whenever something was so forceful that it could not be controlled without the help of a deity, it was itself called a deity."[14] Apart from the major deities the ancients worshiped a number of other powers that, although less vividly realized and perhaps less potent than the great gods, presided over certain branches of social life or nature.

Let us turn to biblical examples of personification! Languages whose grammatical structure gives male or female gender to "things" invite personification. Hebrew is one of those languages. In addition, the Hebrew language has a stylistic preference for nominative constructions and tends to link abstract concepts to action verbs. Instead of saying, "Do not be wicked," the Hebrew may say, "Let not wickedness dwell in your tents [Job 11:14, rsv]"; instead of "He defrauds the workers who build," it says, "[He] builds his house by unrighteousness [Jer. 22:13, rsv]"; instead of "He always forgives," it says, "He is abundant in pardon [Isa. 55:7]." The abstract concept may also become the

132

subject. Instead of "He shall become poor," it says, "Want will come upon him [Prov. 28:22, RSV]." The poet merely has to take the language at its word: plants, inanimate objects, abstractions, cities, and nations can be treated as people in Old Testament poetry. The city of Jerusalem is the "daughter of Zion"; the ruins of the city are called on to rejoice; trees are to sing for joy; righteousness and peace will kiss each other; steadfast love and faithfulness are the companions of Yahweh, and the Law is a servant guarding the children.[15]

Personification enables the poet to speak more clearly and to the point than ordinary, descriptive language would permit. Here is an example from Proverbs 20:1:

> *Wine is a ne'er-do-well,*
> *Beer is a noisy brawler;*
> *None who are swayed by them turn wise.*

Without the poetic embellishment of personification, there would only be a dry warning against drinking. That kind of warning is readily forgotten. But "ne'er-do-well" and "noisy brawler" evoke immediate recollections in the reader's mind of personal experiences with people who drink too much. The memory, imagination, and thought processes are engaged. Here, poetic expression is clearly superior, alleviating the shortcomings of conventional language.

These simple personifications, however, do not exhaust the use of this device in Hebrew rhetoric and poetry. Often more extensive and elaborate personifications are used to illustrate a complex idea or state of affairs. In the fable in Judges 9:8ff. the olive tree, the fig tree, and the vine are given voice to express antiroyal sentiments. The fable becomes a device used in political propaganda. In Ezekiel 16 the people of Israel are personified as a young woman who gives herself to Egyptians, Assyrians, Aramaeans, and "any passer-by"; she does not accept the wages of harlotry and gives children to her foreign lovers. This personification implies metaphorical language that gives the name of harlotry to any form of idolatry. Ezekiel 23 is another example of this kind of language. There, Samaria and Jerusalem are depicted as two sisters, Oholah and Oholibah, respectively,

133

both of whom engage in prostitution, provoking the wrath of Yahweh. Even the girl Babylon has to come down from her royal throne, take off her precious clothes, and do the work of a slave grinding on a millstone.[16] By contrast, God speaks of Jerusalem as a woman who has drunk the cup of wrath and whose sons have been killed. God will change his attitude toward her and turn against her enemies.[17]

Especially impressive is a personification found in Zechariah: Wickedness in the land is a woman who has been confined in a large earthen vessel and is being carried to Babylon, where a temple is being built for her.[18] This passage seems to allude to an exorcistic practice: an evil demon is captured in a vessel or bottle and thus rendered harmless. There may be a psychological reason for taking wickedness to be a woman (and not a man). The poet uses a rare feminine noun for wickedness in order to emphasize that men have wickedness as their partner to which they have been attracted.

Are there also personifications of the second, mythological type in the Bible? In the present biblical text as commonly understood by the modern reader, there are not any characters that belong to the "realm-as-personality" complex. Some of the personifications that seem to be innocent and playful, however, had mythological overtones at one point of their career. The Wickedness of Zechariah seems to have been an evil demon presiding over and perhaps inspiring wicked action. The "daughter of Zion" (i.e., Jerusalem personified as a lady) may have been regarded as a goddess, the spouse of the city god.[19] Wisdom also has a mythological background; she used to be the goddess who presided over the world of the intellect that the ancient Hebrews associated with the scribal art and profession. For practical purposes this background was ignored or forgotten by early Judaism.

According to the *Princeton Encyclopedia of Poetry and Poetics*, "personifications replace mythical figures when rational attitudes supersede the primitive imagination."[20] When mythological personifications are reduced to poetic ones, the reduction is often incomplete, and occasionally, the original divine nature makes itself felt. Thus the playful Egyptian tale of the two brothers, Truth and Falsehood, echoes the mythical battle between the

134

gods Horus and Seth.[21] In the form of Bartholdi's famous statue in New York harbor, Liberty represents a blend of French revolutionary and American dreams; part of her appeal is no doubt due to her anchorage in ancient Roman belief in *Libertas*, "the spirit of the Republican constitution."[22] In an interesting paper Harold Mattingly shows how, in late antiquity, Christian authors contested the divine nature of Roman mythological personifications like *Spes* (Hope), *Pax* (Peace), and *Victoria* (Victory) by either explaining them as mere figures of exalted speech or redefining them as angels who are allowed to act, if only under God's direction and control.[23] The Romans represented Victory as a winged lady carrying a wreath and a palm. The Christians, unable to tolerate the belief in a goddess conferring triumph on her devotees, redefined her as God's Angel of Victory. This kind of redefinition is crucial for understanding Wisdom. Although redefined according to later taste or belief, the new figure retains some of her divine features. We may invent all sorts of personifications, and many poets have done so according to their individual taste and fancy. Figures like Dante Gabriel Rossetti's flame-winged Passion of Love, however, remain pale and shadowy and have to be explained. They lack the dignity, weight, and vitality tradition has lent to personifications that started their career as real deities.[24]

"Shadows alone are left" indeed; but what a vital shadow is Wisdom! Although the rank of deity is denied to her, she has retained a general air of dignity.

When we consider Wisdom as a personification of the *poetic* type, then we have to ask *what* does she personify? In the first place, Wisdom stands for the wisdom teaching with its moral injunctions. But she may also be taken to stand for the book— Proverbs 1—9—which recommends itself. The book is responsible, as it were, for its own appearance before the world. The scroll takes on the character of a handsome and well-groomed young lady of noble descent, determined to mix with others, to be seen in public places, and to attract the attention of all who are strangers to knowledge. To them she offers her lessons, both elementary and advanced, and she is prepared to teach in public—right at the city gate. There she chants her invitation in order to assemble a crowd of uneducated youths. Like any other teacher she selects a well-frequented spot where she can be seen to be engaged in teaching and may expect to become known and attract more pupils. Such an understanding of the personification is not far-fetched, for "wisdom" did become a book title, and in the twenty-fourth chapter of Sirach, Wisdom is identified with a book, the Torah, the Jewish book par excellence.

Understood as a simple personification of the poetic type, Wisdom could be received into the canon of the Jewish Bible without contradicting its monotheistic outlook. An allegorical identification of Wisdom and Torah, or, in Christian tradition, Wisdom and the Christ, could only strengthen her canonical position. Such identifications, however, also caused Wisdom's origin as a deity and her early reinterpretation as a rhetorical or poetical device to be forgotten. Although in the fifth century A.D. the Christian exegete Hadrian could label the Wisdom of Proverbs 8—9 a *prosopopeia* (i.e., a personification), it was not until the sixteenth and seventeenth centuries that poets and scholars began to reconsider this view.[25]

CHAPTER 18

Hypostasis—Wisdom Myth —the Voice of Creation: Three Questionable Categories

Having explained my own view, I am now able to comment on and criticize other approaches to the poems. To discuss all the categories ever used to understand Lady Wisdom is unnecessary. Some approaches, however, either are taken more often than others or have managed to establish themselves in standard reference works on the Old Testament. For this reason it seems advisable to defend my own view as opposed to theirs and explain why I feel that they are questionable, if not positively misleading. The views I will discuss use the concept of hypostasis, reconstruct an allegedly ancient Wisdom myth, or assume that Wisdom, as she addresses humankind, represents the voice of creation or nature.

HYPOSTASIS?

Classic Christian theology has designated Father, Son, and Holy Spirit as three *hypostases* of the one God. In modern religious studies the concept of hypostasis has been adopted to designate such beings as "Name of Yahweh" and "Spirit of God" in the Old Testament, *Shekinah* and Holy Spirit in Judaism, *Spenta Mainyu*

(Bounteous Spirit) and *Armaiti* (Obedience) in the Iranian religion, and the fourteen *Ka* (Utterance, Magic, Power, Splendor etc.) of the Egyptian sun god, Re. We are dealing here with either separate beings (like the Iranian *Spenta Mainyu*) or beings that are ultimately identical with a divinity they belong to or represent vis-à-vis their devotees (like the *Shekinah* or the Sacred Heart of Jesus). The various local manifestations of a deity are also considered hypostases, like *Nossa Senhora da Fatima* and *Our Lady of Knock,* both of whom are one and the same Virgin Mary. Equally, El of Bethel, El Elyon of Jerusalem, and El Roi of Beer-Lahai-Roi are none other than the same god, El. In any case there is a closer connection between the hypostasis and its god than there is between genealogically related gods in, say, the Greek pantheon.[1]

Besides the already mentioned hypostases of Name of Yahweh and Spirit of God, the Old Testament contains a host of other hypostases: Face of Yahweh, Glory of God, Word of God, Blessing and Curse of God, Righteousness of God, Power, Jealousy, Kindness, Faithfulness, Peace, etc. Finally, the Messenger of Yahweh, who is identical with Yahweh, should also be mentioned here.[2] Following A. R. Johnson, these hypostases could be regarded as "extensions of Yahweh's personality."[3] Does Wisdom also belong to the category of hypostases?

Wisdom has persistently been called a hypostasis. It was argued that Wisdom, who appears as a person who talks and acts, is nothing but God's wisdom. For theological reasons, however, she was conceptually separated from God and presented as a person acting on her own.[4] Weber formulates these theological reasons:

> God as the essentially other-worldly being cannot directly associate with creatures or act on them. His action and presence has to be mediated. Whenever it is just a matter of activating or guiding existing forces in nature or in humans, this mediation is carried out by angels. However, when God intends to act creatively in history, when he wishes to make known his special grace, then, according to Jewish theology, hypostases appear who, by the portion of divine power and glory given to them, are empowered to mediate the active

138

presence of God. Although creatures themselves, as representatives of God they have divine attributes. Such middle beings are Metatron, Memra of Jehovah, Shekhinah, Holy Spirit, Bat Kol.[5]

Although this list does not include Wisdom, it seemed easy enough to place her in line with hypostases such as *Shekinah, Holy Spirit,* and so on.[6]

This kind of theology has been related to the Persian religion, whose concept of deity contains numerous hypostases, such as *Armaiti* (Obedience), *Asha* (Righteousness), and *Vohu Manah* (Good Intention). All these beings have been considered aspects of the one God of Zoroastrianism, *Ahura Mazda.* It was asserted that the ancient Iranian religion of Zoroastrianism has influenced Judaism, and Persian hypostases provided the models for the hypostases of Jewish theology.[7]

Today, things are seen differently. Although there is reason to believe that there was an extensive Iranian influence on early Judaism, the Zoroastrian hypostases seem to have remained alien to Jewish thought.[8] The mistake made by earlier scholars, however, was less their assumption of a pervasive Persian influence than their erroneous view concerning the early Jewish concept of God. It is beyond dispute that early Jewish literature has its own, distinctive view of the divine world. Its concept of the heavenly realm includes all kinds of angelic beings with liturgical or cosmic functions. Even Satan has been given some of God's tasks to do. The emphasis here is on God's transcendence and otherness. God has become unapproachable. Although unapproachable, God nevertheless is not alienated from direct contact with the world.[9] People avoid pronouncing the name of God, thus giving substitute terms like *Shekinah, Memra,* and Holy Spirit weight of their own. These hypostases are characteristic of human language about God but are not considered separate beings dwelling in heaven. Their interposition is not required to maintain God's holiness or transcendence and bridge the gap between God and the world. The only exception is the philosophical system of Philo of Alexandria (ca. 13 B.C.–A.D. 50). Under the influence of the Platonic tradition of Greek philosophy, Philo developed the doctrine of a distant God whose "powers" or "powerful agents" *(dunameis)* mediate between him and the world.[10] Thus what has been thought to be true of the entire early Jewish religion actually applies only to Philo's philosophical system. Even Philo, however, does not deny that God can act without the aid of intermediaries. A systematic isolation of God from contact with the sinful material world was unknown before the Gnosticism of late antiquity.

There is, then, no early Jewish theology of hypostases based on a special concept of God. Nevertheless, *Memra* and *Shekinah,* Holy Spirit, etc. may certainly still be regarded as hypostases. Is Wisdom a hypostasis as well?

In the book of Proverbs, Wisdom neither represents an aspect of a deity of higher rank nor does she mediate between Creator and creation. It does not really make sense to say that the passage on Wisdom as a child present at creation is a development of another text stating, "Yahweh by wisdom founded the earth."[11] Equally, to make her God's representative and agent in his dealings with humankind[12] or, more specifically, with kings and rulers, cannot be supported on the basis of Proverbs 8:31, 35 and 8:15–21. An identification of Wisdom with Yahweh, however subtly explained, is not borne out by the poems. Yet this is not to deny that early-Jewish sages may have adopted such a reading, which had more support from their monotheistic creed than from the text inherited from polytheistic times.

The poems on Wisdom originate from a time when hypostases did not play a major role in Israel's way of thinking and religious rhetoric. They must have been composed in preexilic times, when Israel's dominant religion was still polytheistic. Not until the first century B.C. or A.D., when the book of Wisdom was written, do we have evidence of Wisdom as a hypostasis. As far as this book is concerned, it is correct to explain that "Wisdom [Sophia] is a part of the *ego* of the divine personality and reflects several aspects of the richness in God. . . . Her actions are none other than God's himself. The author, therefore, ascribes the very same activities to God and to his Wisdom."[13] Only with difficulty can this be asserted of Wisdom as she is represented in the poems of Proverbs.

A WISDOM MYTH?

Some scholars have suggested that the poems on Wisdom are disintegrated fragments of an old and perhaps extra-Israelite Wisdom Myth.[14] They claim that the poems can be understood only if one is familiar with this myth, since the parts are explainable only with reference to the whole structure. The myth is said to have the following plot: Wisdom is of heavenly origin. One day she descended from heaven to earth, desiring to dwell among humans. She was rejected, however, and in resignation returned to her celestial abode.

Given the outline of the myth, the poems are arranged as follows. Proverbs 8 was understood as an account of the celestial origin of Wisdom and as her appeal to be received on earth. Proverbs 9 represents the invitation of Wisdom, the attempt to recruit a following among men. Proverbs 1:20ff., finally, is to be understood as Wisdom's rebuke, her "farewell sermon"[15] before returning to her original heavenly abode. Proverbs 9, however, could not as easily be integrated into the structure of the myth. According to Proverbs 9:1–3, it appears that Wisdom actually has a home among humans. This problem is solved by explaining that there were at least some people who followed Wisdom's invitation—not to a banquet (this is but an image), but to conjugal union.[16] From here, it is argued, the flow of tradition leads to the Wisdom of Solomon, a first-century B.C. work in which conjugal union with Wisdom (*Sophia*) plays an important role. Another text belonging to the same trajectory is Sirach 24, in which the original myth is reworked: Wisdom has eventually found a dwelling among humans, and this is Israel. The various stands of the Wisdom Myth tradition finally converge in Gnostic speculation, which further develops the myth in manifold ways. In Gnostic thought the motif of the otherworldly, celestial origin of Wisdom is given a prominent place and is expanded into a theogony and cosmogony. It is an axiom of Gnostic teaching that individual "gnostics," unlike the masses of ordinary people, are the ones who accept Wisdom's message. Thus Wisdom's message to men is not missing in the Gnostic version of the myth.

The reconstruction of a Wisdom Myth with several variants

and adaptations enabled research to derive many motifs of the sapiential, apocalyptic, Gnostic, and early Christian traditions from one common source—the Wisdom Myth. Thus a picture of imposing consistency could emerge and provide an almost natural explanation of the origins of Gnostic mythology. Of course, this view stands and falls with the factual question of the actual existence of such an ancient Wisdom Myth. A critical analysis of the relevant textual evidence yields the result that in antiquity *there has never been such a Wisdom Myth.* The idea is a mere invention and construction of modern scholarship.[17] We have to abandon this construction, together with several other equally alleged myths—that of an *Urmensch* and of a "Redeemed Redeemer." The history-of-religions school, on which the reconstruction of our Wisdom Myth depends, had a distinct tendency to develop these kinds of assumptions. None of them has stood the test of recent criticism.

The clearest support for the alleged Wisdom Myth was a poem about Wisdom and Iniquity. The poem is found in the book of Enoch (chapter 42), an apocryphal work probably dating from the first century A.D. The poem reads as follows:

> *Wisdom could not find a place in which she could dwell;*
> *but a place was found for her in the heavens.*
> *When Wisdom went out to dwell with the children of the*
> *people,*
> *she found no dwelling place.*
> *[So] Wisdom returned to her place*
> *and settled permanently among the angels.*
> *Then Iniquity went out of her rooms,*
> *and found whom she did not expect.*
> *And she dwelt with them,*
> *like rain in a desert,*
> *like dew on a thirsty land.[18]*

Here, Wisdom and Iniquity are contrasted with each other. Wisdom finds no place among humans, but Iniquity is welcomed "like rain in a desert, like dew on a thirsty land."[19] The poem is a charge against Iniquity reminiscent of prophetic language in the Old Testament (Isaiah 59:14):

142

Justice is rebuffed and flouted
while Righteousness stands aloof;
Truth stumbles in the market-place
and Honesty is kept out of court,
so Truth is lost to sight.[20]

The poem personifies Wisdom and is therefore in keeping with the early Jewish tradition. As in Proverbs 9, the personification is contrasted with an opposing figure, Iniquity. Here, Iniquity, meaning lawlessness or apostasy from the Jewish Law, takes the place of Folly. Moreover, Wisdom here denotes the Torah (i.e., the Jewish Law). While Proverbs 9 would be misunderstood as echoing the conflict between Jewish Law and apostasy, a correct explanation of the poem in Enoch cannot do without these categories. Another difference is equally obvious: the setting of Enoch 42 is quite different from that of Proverbs 9. The scene is no longer the public square in town, but the whole cosmos, including heaven and earth. Wisdom descends from heaven and returns to heaven. Iniquity falls like rain from the chambers of the clouds. This cosmic framework is characteristic of apocalyptic literature of which the book of Enoch is an example.

Perhaps Wisdom's return to heaven can be explained more adequately. The motif is neither an invention of the poet nor an elaboration of an older prophetic motif (the absence of Truth and Justice from the country), but has probably been inspired by a well-known Greek myth. The myth tells of a "good goddess" who leaves the land because of human wickedness and retreats to Mount Olympus and her father, Zeus. In Hesiod, this myth concerns two goddesses called *Aidos* (Respect) and *Nemesis* (Just Retribution), in Theognis *Pistis* (Trust) and *Sophrosune* (Prudence), while Aratos mentions only one figure, *Dike* (Justice). After these goddesses have retired to heaven, humankind is left with misfortune and evil.[21] When wickedness prevailed among men, then "*Dike,* filled with hate for the human race, flew toward heaven and there took her residence, where still at night she shows herself to men."[22]

It seems obvious: There is no trace here of an ancient Wisdom Myth that supposedly has been adapted to Jewish ideas by adding the figure of Iniquity, as one scholar has inferred.[23] The

143

poem of the book of Enoch adapts a Greek myth that is different from all Gnostic, early Christian, and cabalistic mythologies and should not be confused with them. Consequently, the Enochic poem has no bearing whatsoever on the understanding of Wisdom as she appears in the biblical book of Proverbs.

THE LANGUAGE OF CREATION?

Gerhard von Rad quite correctly observes that while many authors have explored the origins of Wisdom in the history of religions, Wisdom's significance in Israelite thought has been neglected.[24] At the same time von Rad assumes that the poets were indebted to Egyptian models. The poems were created, he explains, by "cosmopolitan wisdom teachers who had been greatly stimulated by their contact with the wisdom of foreign nations" (175). According to him, Proverbs 8 uses Egyptian motifs and forms of speech (153f.). It was especially in the term *hokmah*, wisdom, that the Israelite teachers found an equivalent to the Egyptian goddess Maat (155, n. 12). All this, however, is relatively insignificant. "More interesting," explains von Rad, "than their [Israel's intellectuals'] dependence on this stimulus is surely their independent theological achievement" (175). Moreover, at the decisive point, the parallelism of *hokmah* and Maat breaks down: The notion that Maat would actually speak to human beings is foreign to the Egyptians. Yet the basic concept of Israel's teachers was precisely that of having Wisdom address humans (174). More specifically, the "doctrine of the self-manifesting primeval order" (170), "the idea of a testimony emanating from creation is attested only in Israel"; it stands "on a genuinely Israelite basis" (175).

The idea of order, too, must be genuinely Israelite rather than borrowed. It may indeed be genuinely human. "One certainly cannot imagine," explains von Rad, "that this doctrine was uttered one day for the first time by an original mind, or even that it was taken over from Egypt. Its roots are old, even within Israel" (170). Sapiential thought has always been persuaded that there is "a great all-embracing order including everything that exists" (154), for Yahweh has ordered his creation wisely; indeed, he has "poured out" wisdom over his creation.[25] This wisely

144

established primal order manifests itself to humanity: the birds of the air, the plants of the earth, and the fish of the sea are teaching of the creator, and the heavens proclaim God's righteousness.[26]

From there, it is only a small step to Wisdom calling on human beings with a promise of knowledge, understanding, success, riches, etc. In writing about Wisdom's voice, the teachers "have unquestionably exposed an aspect of creative reality with which Yahwism had not yet concerned itself" (165). They give voice to a form of revelation that, not without tension, was to take its place beside the language of ritual, the narratives of Yahweh's deeds in history, and the voice of the prophets. According to von Rad.

Departing from all previous interpretations, von Rad seeks a fresh approach to the poems on Wisdom. He is right in noting that the Israelites knew what can be called "the silent language of things." The examples of this are in fact much more numerous than von Rad seems to suggest. Here are some more examples:

> *Three things are never satisfied;*
> *four never say, "Enough":*
> *Sheol, the barren womb [of a woman],*
> *the earth ever thirsty for water,*
> *and the fire which never says, "Enough."*
> > —*Proverbs 30:15–16*, RSV

> *The night which said, "A man-child is conceived."*
> > —*Job 3:3*, RSV

> *The deep says, "It [wisdom] is not in me," . . .*
> *The abyss and death say, "Just a rumor we have heard of her."*
> > —*Job 28:14, 22*

> *The stone will cry out from the wall,*
> *and the beam from the woodwork respond.*
> > —*Habakkuk 2:11*, RSV

> *If these [the disciples of Jesus] were silent, the very stones would cry out.*
> > —*Luke 19:40*, RSV

145

Passages in extrabiblical sources also show that knowledge of the "language of things" was widespread. A Ugaritic example: "I have a tale that I would tell you, a word that I would repeat to you, a tale of trees and a whisper of stones, the sighing of the heavens to the earth, of the oceans to the stars."[27] Another example can be found in Augustine's *Confessions* (10:6): "I asked the sea, the depths, the creeping things among living animals, and they replied: We are not thy God; look above us." And, finally, Shakespeare, *As You Like It* (2:1): "[Life] finds tongues in trees . . . sermons in stone."

We cannot help but hear the "language of things." But is this language also the basis of Wisdom represented as a person who addresses human beings? Yes and no. Yes, to the extent that poetry personifies things into speaking subjects. No, to the extent that Wisdom is more than a simple embodiment of creation or the ordering principle of reality, for Wisdom, as a goddess, as well as a goddess reinterpreted, clearly stands *above* the created world.

CHAPTER 19

Lady Wisdom in Church, Speculation, and Mysticism

The figure of Lady Wisdom has a rich and varied history in Jewish and Christian traditions. Few biblical texts have asserted as strong an influence on theology, mysticism, and poety as the poems on Wisdom. What are the reasons for Wisdom's success? Why has Wisdom not been forgotten?

THE APPEAL OF VAGUENESS

Surprisingly, her vagueness and elusiveness provide a first answer. Regardless of whether she is presented as lover, teacher, or goddess, Wisdom remains a fairly vague figure. The poet describes neither her appearance nor her features, clothing, and so on; nor does he say anything about her age. It is left to the reader, ancient and modern, to imagine what she looks like. That the poet refuses to depict his subject for us, thus greatly stimulating our imagination, is not at all surprising but rather the norm in biblical literature. Nowhere do we learn what Moses, King Solomon, Jesus, or Peter looked like. Even Samson's famous long hair is only implied but not actually described in the story.[1] Except for the Song of Songs, the only descriptions of persons found in the Bible are those of David, Absalom, and Elijah. "He was ruddy, and had beautiful eyes, and was handsome [1 Sam. 16:12, rsv]." "In all Israel there was no one so much to be praised for his beauty as Absalom; from the sole of his foot to the crown of his head there was no blemish in him" (with the following verse adding a reference to Absalom's thick hair).[2] Of the prophet Elijah we are simply informed that "he wore a garment of haircloth, with a girdle of leather about his loins [2 Kings 1:8, rsv]." The remaining reports are even scantier. Saul was a head taller than the others, and the prophet Elisha was bald.[3]

By contrast, the literature of classic antiquity includes the literary portrait as a firmly established genre. "Bowlegged, with one limping leg, and shoulders rounded above his chest, he had a skull quite conical, and mangy fuzz like mold." Thus Homer describes the ugly cynic Thersites.[4] In his *Lives of the Caesars* Suetonius describes the appearance of the Roman emperors as a matter of course. Diogenes Laertius knows what some of the Greek philosophers looked like.[5] In Lucian's satirical *Images* two men are arguing about the looks of an incomparable woman, and Tacitus offers a description of his father-in-law, Aratus: "Should those who come after us want to know his appearance, he was well-proportioned rather than slim; there was no passion in his face; his dominant feature was the winning graciousness of his countenance."[6]

Not only literary portraits are missing from the Bible. We can look in vain for landscape descriptions, which are even more commonly found in classical literature. In the Bible the spoken word and the active deed are dominant. People as well as countries are known by their "fruits,"[7] rather than by their outward appearance. Thus Joshua's scouts returned from Canaan not with maps, but with the fruit of the land. The Bible shares this peculiar characteristic with other early literature, such as the Old English or Old Norse writings.[8] Only postbiblical literature has given external features and an individual appearance to biblical personalities. The earliest example of this is a description of Paul in the *Acts of Paul,* dating from the late second century A.D.: "He saw Paul coming, a small man of stature, with a bald head and crooked legs, of noble bearing, his eyebrows grown together, and a somewhat prominent nose, full of friendliness."[9] What we have here is a sketch of Paul as an ugly but friendly migrant philosopher, cast in the image of Socrates!

It goes without saying that modern novelists, in developing biblical plots, regularly furnish their characters with definite features. While, according to the biblical text, "the maiden was very beautiful," Joseph Heller presents David's concubine in graphic detail:

> Abishag the Shunammite is a comely, tidy girl of a yielding and obedient nature and quiet, graceful motions. . . . She is slight and delicate in body and very young, with a smooth and dusky complexion, glossy, straight black hair combed back and downward and rolling outward at her shoulders into an even curl, and very large, meek inviting eyes with huge whites and dark irises that are almost the shade of ebony.[10]

The distance between the laconic assertion of beauty and the detail supplied by modern fiction is striking and indicative of a new, modern sensibility.

The vague picture of biblical personalities is one of the reasons why the iconography of biblical illustrations has been subject to constant change. This is also true of the iconography of Wisdom, for it is left entirely to the imagination of readers or artists whether they fancy her a grown woman (decision of most artists) or a small child (Michelangelo in the Sistine Chapel of the Vatican).[11] We are not even told that she is beautiful, although we may take beauty for granted in the case of a goddess. In Egypt, Ugarit, and Greece, female beauty has often been compared with the beauty of goddesses.[12] A remark by Paul Claudel illuminates how far the imagination does range in conjuring up images of Wisdom. Claudel found Proverbs 8 such fascinating reading that there are no female characters in his writings, he asserts, who do not bear some of the features of Wisdom.[13] Specifically, what these features are he does not tell us; they are features of his imagination. Conversely, Jane Leade, an English mystic of the seventeenth century, has left us a description of Wisdom. To her, she appeared as a woman "most preciously adorned with transparent gold. Her hair fell down onto her shoulders, and her face shone like a brightly shining crystal, her eyes being lovely and kind."[14] Here, the image has been shaped in bold, visual terms. To the Hebrews, however, action was more impressive than vision. Therefore, the Hebrew poet's bold allusion to Wisdom's embraces as a lover[15] must remain vague and cannot develop into actual description.

The success of the Wisdom motif was not exclusively linked to that of the Bible. To put it more precisely, the success and influence of the Wisdom motif is more broadly based than that of the Bible and the book of Proverbs. Wisdom has asserted her independence and has, as it were, emigrated from the book of Proverbs. The ties have been severed that connected the wisdom of the ancient Israelite school (whose image Wisdom was intended to be) to the image as such. The label turned out to be more successful than the product. At first, there remained a certain kinship between Wisdom and the book of Proverbs; Sirach 24, for instance, imitated the poem of Proverbs 8, substituting the Torah (i.e., the Jewish Law) for the older wisdom teaching. In the book of Wisdom, Wisdom *(Sophia)* is already further removed from her original meaning in Proverbs. Here, she supports the Israelites on their way through history as an image of divine assistance. In Gnostic and mystical writings, almost no connection with the book of Proverbs can be found. There, Wisdom serves as a cipher to metaphysical realities and the interpretation of mystical experience. Wisdom turned into an ontological scheme that may be used to interpret reality and reflect on the relationship between the human and the divine.

There is, however, yet another reason for Wisdom's incomparable success: the persistent use of the Bible in theology, liturgy, preaching, and piety. For Wisdom did not just emigrate from the Bible; she continued to be present in the Bible as well. Christians and Jews are under constant obligation to read and interpret the Bible. Because the Bible continues to be a living source, the interpretation of the ancient biblical poems has been persistently influenced by the historical fortunes of the "emigrated" Wisdom motif. A mystic reads the Bible differently than a cabalist does, and again, a Gnostic would prefer readings that differ from those adopted or favored by conventional theology. The result has been a strange interpenetration of exegesis; of learned, pious, and mystical images; of philosophical concepts and speculations. The poem of Sirach 24, for instance, imitates Proverbs 8 but shows no intention of interpreting Proverbs 8. Nevertheless, Sirach 24 has influenced the interpretation of Proverbs 8 to the extent that even in the older poem, Wisdom has been taken to mean the Torah. This kind of transference has been aided by the allegorical method of precritical exegesis.

This is not the place to retrace the intertwined paths of Wisdom in the history of biblical exegesis and imagination that goes beyond the Bible. Yet it may be helpful to identify the major ways of dealing with the motif. Three distinct categories can be distinguished: protological-soteriological, ontological, and mystical.

WISDOM IN CREATION AND SALVATION

Wisdom, who speaks demanding obedience, inviting love, and promising salvation, could readily be identified with the Torah. For Christians, it was considerably more difficult to identify Wisdom with Christ. While Wisdom of the book of Proverbs has generally taken on the meaning of Torah in Jewish sources,[16] there are few and not very explicit references to an identification of Christ and *Sophia* in the New Testament.[17] On the basis of Proverbs 8:22 Judaism developed a doctrine of the preexistence of the Torah, and Christianity taught the preexistence of Christ *before* creation. For the doctrine of the Torah's existence before the world was created, Proverbs 8 served as a prooftext: "Nine hundred and forty-seven years before the creation of the world, the Torah had already been written; she lay in the bosom of the Holy One—may he be praised—and sang with the ministering angels; as it is said, *I was beside him* [Prov. 8:30]."[18] Jewish exegesis also related Proverbs 8:22 to Genesis 1:1 and developed a doctrine of the mediating role of the Torah in creation—a doctrine that found its counterpart in the Christian doctrine that gave Christ a mediating role in creation.[19] In the oldest layers of tradition there are only rare traces of a Wisdom Christology. The Synoptic Q source has a passage that subordinates Jesus to Wisdom, making him her messenger:

Therefore also the Wisdom of God said, "I will send them prophets (and wise men and scribes?), and some of them they will kill and persecute, that the blood of all the prophets shed from the foundation of the world may be required of this generation, from the blood of Abel to the blood of Zechariah, who perished between the altar and the sanctuary. (Amen?) I tell you, it will be required of this generation."[20]

Whereas Luke's Gospel (Luke 11:49–50) cites the passage almost literally, Matthew (Matthew 23:34–36) attributes these words to Jesus.[21]

This, however, is an isolated case. A distinct Wisdom Christology cannot be found until the church fathers. In the second century Justin identifies Christ with the Wisdom of Proverbs 8, and in the third century this reading is found in the oldest surviving biblical commentaries.[22] In the controversies over the Arian Christology, both parties sought to legitimate their positions with Proverbs 8 as a prooftext, although the Arians, no doubt, had the advantage with their conception of the creation of Christ. At any rate, by the fourth century Proverbs 8 had become a classic text in the christological debate. Consequently, hardly a thought was given to the view that Wisdom represented the Holy Spirit.[23] The christological interpretation of Lady Wisdom had been firmly established.

From the seventh century onward the poems Sirach 24 and Proverbs 8 have been used as liturgical readings at holy days celebrating the Virgin Mary. They have been regarded as texts about the birth of Christ of Mary, his mother. The birth of Christ in history corresponds to the birth of Christ before all history. In his famous bull *Ineffabilis Deus* of 1854, Pius IX explains this relationship somewhat differently. He asserts that the Wisdom texts refer primarily to Christ, yet to Mary as well because her birth "was ordained by the same decree as the incarnation of Divine Wisdom [i.e., Christ]." From the eleventh century, Mary herself has also been regarded as Wisdom and given the status of something like a fourth person in the Trinity. There is an especially charming scene in a late medieval song that gives Mary a seat and voice in the council of the Trinity and has her take part in a discussion of the forthcoming creation.[24]

The dominant interpretation, however, continued to be the

152

one identifying Wisdom with Christ. The most extensive mariological commentary on the Wisdom poems, written by the Spaniard F. Q. de Salazar (1637), gives an equal amount of space to the christological interpretation. Identifying *Sophia* with Mary, therefore, is but a variation of the christological reading. This is true also of yet another view, the rather daring identification of Sophia with the church as the Body of Christ.[25] In his little-known musical mystery play, *La Sagesse ou La parabole du festin,* Paul Claudel presents Wisdom as the church inviting the people. He combines the parable of the rejected invitation to the wedding feast (Luke 14) with the Wisdom poems in a sophisticated and rather attractive way.[26]

Wisdom, interpreted either as Christ or as Torah, thus became the key to the way of salvation, a way that had been ordained before creation. That Wisdom became a code word for an official Christian or orthodox Jewish theology can also be seen in the fact that Folly, as Wisdom's opponent, became a symbol for deviance and heresy.[27]

WISDOM IN METAPHYSICAL SPECULATION

Wisdom also plays a part in a number of Gnostic, cabalistic, and idealist ontologies. In many Gnostic ontologies *Sophia* is seen as one of the thirty beings belonging to the divine world.[28] According to a Gnostic myth, without a man, Sophia produced a child that was born as a miscarriage. The child, called Yaldabaoth, created the world as well as humankind.[29] This appears to be a reworked version of a Jewish myth that spoke of Wisdom participating in the creation of the world.[30] There are quite a few versions of this myth. Some of them introduce a second Wisdom figure, *Akhamoth;* she is a daughter of Sophia and functions as the mother of the creator of the world.[31] One of the versions of this Gnostic ontology appears in the Jewish cabala. *Hokmah,* in cabalistic thought, is one of the ten creative potencies emanating from God. Here, the oldest source is the *Sepher Yeṣirah,* probably dating from the third century A.D. In the Christian cabala of the seventeenth century, *hokmah* gained special significance by being identified with Christ. A more common view was that Wisdom

153

(Christ) carried within her (him) the entire Platonic world of ideas as a blueprint of creation. Proverbs 8 is the source for a Platonizing doctrine of creation not only for the church fathers, but also for modern neoscholasticism.[32] Traditional textbooks of Catholic dogma also discuss Proverbs 8 under the heading "Traces of the three-personhood of God in the Old Testament." This kind of speculation received an unexpected upgrading when, in the new Roman lectionary of 1969, Proverbs 8:22–31 made its appearance as a reading for the Feast of the Trinity. A homiletic journal commented on this text: "In the context of this feast, the text causes problems. Most expository sermons which use this text looking for Old Testament support of the doctrine of the Trinity, appear to be dragging it in by the heels."[33] No doubt the same judgment applies to the exegesis underlying this choice of a pericope. Responsible preaching, rather, would see in Proverbs 8 an illustration of the variety of the biblical understanding of God and the divine world. Human wisdom does not stand by itself. To the sensitive person it may disclose itself as a sacred reality, as reality grounded in the divine. Because God is never far from the world and from the marketplace, not just human but also divine wisdom may be found there. *C'est qu'en écoutant les sages on entend plus qu'eux.*[34]

In the history of mysticism Wisdom has always aroused speculative interest, as in Boehme and Solovyev, for instance. As a rule, however, the mystical trend has been dominant over speculative interest. It is therefore more appropriate to sketch the mystical understanding of Wisdom than to pursue the fuzzy notions of mystical ontologies.

WISDOM IN MYSTICISM

Christian mysticism has consistently made use of the biblical texts on Wisdom to help interpret the mystical experience. Such spirituality is deeply rooted in early sources and can be extensively documented from the book of Wisdom and Philo.[35] Among Christians one of the primary theological understandings of asceticism was a spiritual marriage with the Divine Savior. Origen, for instance, considered the human soul (Greek *psuche*, fem.) as Christ's bride.[36] Others perceived Christ in feminine

154

terms, approaching her as Sophia or Wisdom. The Dominican mystic Henry Suso (d. 1366) was probably the first to do so. In his autobiography he tells how, at his monastery in Constance, passages from the book of Proverbs were read at mealtime to the community. Shortly afterward, Wisdom appeared to him in a vision. He describes her as follows:

> She was floating high above him [Suso] on a tower of clouds, resplendent like the morning star, bright as a blinking star. Her crown was eternity, her garment bliss, her word loveliness, her embrace fulfillment of all desire. She was far and yet near, exalted and lowly, present yet also concealed. She let herself be touched, yet no one could grasp her. She towered above the highest heights of the heavens and touched God's deepest abyss. She stretched mightily from end to end ordering all things with kindness. Now, she seemed to him [Suso] a lady, young and noble, then in an instant, he saw a proud, young squire; now her manner was that of a wise mistress, then that of a beautiful lover.[37]

Wisdom became Suso's mystical spouse. The section of his autobiography containing the passage just quoted is entitled "How he came to spiritual matrimony with Eternal Wisdom." Such mystical marriages seem to have flourished in certain circles. In the 1660s a certain Claude Martin entered into a marriage with Wisdom with a written document (which he burned).[38] This constitutes the beginning of a rich mystical tradition associated with such names as Jacob Boehme (d. 1710), Johann Georg Gichtel (d. 1710), Jane Leade (d. 1704), Gottfried Arnold (d. 1717), Louis Marie Grignion (d. 1716), and Vladimir Solovyev (d. 1900). Solovyev is the founder of so-called sophiology, also known as Russian Gnosticism, a school of thought that is not primarily speculative in nature, but carries the firm imprint of the mystical. Solovyev himself encountered the Holy Sophia in a vision he had in the desert near Cairo, Egypt, in November 1875.[39] Teilhard de Chardin's hymn *"L'éternel féminin"* (1918), with its clear reference to Proverbs 8 may also have been influenced by Russian sophiology:

> *When the world was born, I came into being.*
> *Before the centuries were made,*

155

I issued from the hand of God . . .
I am the beauty running through the world,
To make it associate in ordered groups:
The ideal held up before the world
To make it ascend.
I am the essential Feminine.[40]

Given this variety of interpretation it is not surprising that the original meaning of the poems on Wisdom got lost. Yet, in a gradual process, their original meaning has been recovered again by critical research.

NOTES

CHAPTER 1: *Introduction: Wisdom, Polytheism, and the Hebrew School*

1. In Boening 1977:425.
2. Gunkel 1903:26.
3. von Rad 1972:144.
4. Lang 1972:46–60; esp. 55ff.
5. Jer. 44:18; cf. Heimpel 1982:71.
6. Sartre 148:54f. Cf. Iser 1978:107ff; Fish 1980.
7. The following "difficult" linguistic and stylistic features have often misled scholars to making textual emendations or postulating revisions of the original text: (a) Hendiadys. "At the gates of the city, at the entrance of the portals" (Prov. 8:3), for instance, is a poetic expression for "at the city gate." Hendiadys pairs are often joined together in the construct state, cf. Prov. 1:27 *(sh'wh phdkm)*; 8:12 *(dᶜt mzmwt)*, 31 *(tbl 'rṣw)*. This important stylistic feature is discussed in Avishur, 1984 (esp. 157, 161, 244). (b) The expression "to chisle *(hṣb)* pillars [Prov. 9:1]" is quite correct, see the paired words chisle/build in Prov. 9:1; Deut. 6:10f.; *Exod. Rab.* 15:22 to Exod. 12:12. Cf. Daiches 1943/44. (c) In Prov. 1:20; 8:3 *taronnah* "she chants" is a *forma energica*, cf. van der Weiden 1970:63. (d) Prov. 1:22–23, 27; 8:13, 29–30, 34 have the tricolon verse form that is also used elsewhere in the same collection (Prov. 5:19; 6:3, 22). Only Prov. 8:13a seems to be a gloss. (e) The expressions "she makes her speech" *('mryh t'mr)* Prov. 1:21 and "behold" *(hnh)* stand outside the metric structure. For this so-called anacrusis cf. Robinson

1936; Cross 1974; Parker 1974:283. (f) The change from the second to the third person in Prov. 1:22a/bc and 1:27/28 is a stylistic device, cf. Gevirtz 1973:170f; Lohfink 1981:51.

8. Voltaire 1828:306.
9. Köhler 1953:46.
10. According to Nachtigal 1799, not only Proverbs, but also Song of Songs, Koheleth, and Wisdom originated in the ancient Israelite academies.
11. Renan 1953:609.
12. Sayce 1908:51.
13. Cf. the *Instruction of Amenemope* (ANET 421–424; Lichtheim 2:146–163) with Prov. 22:17—23:11; Bryce 1979.
14. *The Times* (London) of May 26, 1938.
15. Cf. Lemaire 1981:94–95, n. 73–75.
16. This view has recently been repeated by McKane 1983.
17. Sanders 1972:113f.
18. Koch (1955) 1983; Gerstenberger 1965; Barr 1966.
19. Lang 1980; Lemaire 1981 and 1984.
20. The basis of modern estimates is the British census of Palestine of 1922, which counted a total number of around 757,000 inhabitants.
21. Smith 1973:394.
22. W. F. Albright in Kraeling/Adams 1960:122. Cf. the discussion in Lang 1980:108ff.
23. Schmid 1974:21. Similar views can be found all over the world. Hölderlin the poet found them in Hesiod; Hegel the philosopher referred to Confucius (Hölderlin 1961; Hegel 1923:315).
24. Kant 1:984.
25. Schiller, translated in Boening 1977:329.
26. 1 Kings 3.
27. Isa. 31:2.
28. Caquot 1978:25. For examples see Exod. 31:3f; Prov. 24:3; 1 Kings 3:28; Koh. 10:10.
29. For *sophia*, cf. Wisd. 14:2; Homer, *Iliad* 15:412; Plato, *Protagoras* 321d; Burford 1972:208ff. For *wisheit*, cf. Schmitt-Fiack 1972, Francke 1972.
30. Caquot 1978:25f. (quoting M. Detienne, J.-P. Vernant).
31. McKane 1970.
32. Prov. 1:22.
33. Chase 1944:239f.

CHAPTER 3. *Street, Square, Gate*

1. Prov. 8:1ff.; 9:3.
2. Jer. 5:1; 7:17; etc.
3. Jer. 33:10.
4. Jer. 9:20.
5. 1 Kings 20:34. The *Revised Standard Version* has "bazaars."
6. Isa. 15:3; Amos 5:16.
7. Isa. 42:2.
8. Lam. 2:19.
9. Lam. 4:14f.
10. Jer. 11:6. Cf. Luke 10:10; 13:26; Josephus, *War* 6:301.
11. Mic. 7:10; Zech. 9:3; etc.
12. Job 18:17.
13. 2 Sam. 1:20.
14. Jer. 44:9.
15. Gen. 19:1f.; 2 Chron. 32:6; Neh. 8:1.
16. Esth. 4:6.
17. Ezra 10:9.
18. Job 29.
19. Job 29:12–17; 2 Chron. 29:4; 32:6; Neh. 8:1ff.
20. Esth. 6:9ff.; 2 Sam. 21:12.
21. Isa. 15:3; Jer. 48:38; etc.
22. Judg. 19:15ff.
23. Isa. 59:14; Jer. 5:1f.; Ps. 55:12.
24. Jer. 9:20; Zech. 8:4f.
25. Gen. 22:17; 1 Kings 8:37; etc.
26. Herzog 1976:xvii.
27. Aharoni 1973:406f.
28. Herzog 1976:xx.
29. Amos 5:15.
30. Job 29.
31. Gibson 1977:107 (ANET 151). Smith 1952:45: "One of the regular features in Arab villages or small towns is the meeting on the threshing-floor, the best place generally available."
32. Gen. 23:10; 34:20; Ruth 4:1.
33. 2 Kings 7:1; cf. Neh. 13:15–22.
34. Prov. 31:23; Lam. 5:14; cf. Ezek. 11:1f.
35. Ps. 69:13.
36. Exod. 32:26; 2 Sam. 19:9; 1 Kings 22:11; 2 Chron. 32:6; Neh. 8:1.
37. Jer. 17:19; 19:2.

159

38. Deut. 21:19; Jer. 26:10; Prov. 22:22; etc. Cf. Köhler 1953: 145–59; Macholz 1972:317f.; Frick 1977:116–27.
39. Gen. 23:10, 18; Prov. 5:14; 26:26. Cf. Speiser 1967: 83–88; Evans 1962/63.
40. Prov. 7:12; 9:14.
41. Reported in a newspaper (*Reutlinger Generalanzeiger* of Dec. 4, 1973).
42. Lindblom 1925:114.
43. Jer. 17:19–27; 19:1–13. There was also an unorthodox sanctuary at the Joshua Gate of Jerusalem (2 Kings 23:8).
44. Cicero, *The Orator* 3:133f. (after Cicero 1970:230).
45. Job 29:24f.
46. For the Hebrew "palaver" *(sod)* see Köhler 1953:89ff.
47. Prov. 24:32.
48. Prov. 7:6.
49. Goebel 1932:181.
50. Meissner 2:327 for ancient Mesopotamia; similarly, Williams 1972:216 for Egypt.
51. Augustine, *Confessions* 1:16. Cf. Bonner 1977:115–25.
52. Augustine, *Confessions* 1:16.
53. Dio Chrysostom, quoted in Bonner 1977:116.
54. Livy, *Roman History* 3:44,6; Augustine, *Confessions* 1:13.
55. Aeschines, *Against Timarchos* 12.
56. Bonner 1973:527. See the illustration in Bonner 1977:118.
57. Nilsson 1955:61.
58. Talmud, b. Mo‛ed Qat. 16b. For outdoor teaching in Talmudic times see Dimitrowsky 1976:333–42.
59. Midr. Qoh. 1:7.
60. Cf. Talmud, b. Ber. 24b and b. Meg. 28a.
61. Talmud, b. Pesaḥ. 112a.

CHAPTER 4. *The Rhetoric of Teaching*
1. Cf. Prov. 21:16, 25.
2. Brunner 1957:57ff., 174ff. For thrashing in the Bible cf. Prov. 13:24; 22:15.
3. Prov. 3:1f. RSV. Cf. Prov. 4:4, 20ff.; 7:1f.; Sir. 51:23–26.
4. The many contacts between Egyptian instruction literature and Proverbs allow us to use Brunner 1957:32–38, 126–31 for reconstructing the image of the Israelite teacher.
5. Heinze 1960:43–58.

160

6. Bollnow 1958:107.
7. Eliot 1980:49, in his essay on "Tradition and Individual Talent."
8. 2 Kings 10:1; 1 Chron. 27:32.
9. Arzt 1953:39–43. According to Isa. 49:23, the task of teaching young children is degrading for foreign kings and queens who have lost their office and rank.
10. Cf. 2 Sam. 17.
11. This is the meaning of "to seek" in Prov. 1:28. The same verb, *shḥr* pi., means, in Sir. 6:36, "to visit (the teacher in his home)." Westermann 1974:167ff. discusses to seek— to find as metaphors for intellectual activities.
12. Cf. Job 23:8f.; Amos 8:12.
13. Cf. Deut. 1:45; Judg. 10:12f.; 1 Sam. 28:15; Job 35:12; etc.
14. Prov. 4:1; 5:1; Deut. 27:9; Judg. 9:7; Acts 19:33f.
15. Cf. Cicero, *Against Catilina* 1:1 (quousque tandem) and Lausberg 1960:§767–70.
16. Exod. 10:3; 1 Kings 18:21; Josh. 18:3; Job 8:2; 18:2; 19:2.
17. Sir. 51:24 (not the beginning of a speech).
18. Lang 1972:33f.; Whedbee 1971:54, 75–79. For examples see Prov. 1:17ff.; 2:21f.; 3:32–35; Isa. 14:27; 28:29; Ps. 1:6.
19. Sophocles, *Ajax* 131f. and *Antigone* 326. Cf. Lausberg 1960:§879.
20. Prov. 3:1f., 21–26; 4:4, 20ff.; Ps. 34:12f.; Deut. 4:1; Isa. 55:1–5.
21. Gevirtz 1973:170f.
22. Trible 1975:516f.

CHAPTER 5. *Brief Commentary on Proverbs 1:20–33*
1. *Ḥokmot* is in the plural as in Prov. 9:1; 14:1; Sir. 4:11. Some scholars identify it as a Canaanite singular (van der Weiden 1970:85f.).
2. "At the head of the busy street" is a conjectural rendering accepted by most recent translators (JPS, Plöger 1984). Others follow the Septuagint by proposing a slight emendation (read *ḥomiyot,* a Canaanite plural form; Dahood 1963:4f.):"on top of the walls."
3. Cf. Jer. 22:20; Judg. 9:7 for Hebrew *qara'*.
4. Cf. Isa. 12:6; Ps. 59:17; 107:22.
5. The Egyptian *Instruction Addressed to King Merikare* refers to a former classmate of the king as "a man whose virtues

161

you know, with whom you once *chanted* the writings" (Lichtheim 1:100f.).

6. Literally, "mischief-makers, they indeed *(lhm)* delight in mischief-making." Cf. Whitley 1974/75:228.
7. Verse 23 and Ps. 78:1f. share the same rhetorical pattern. Some expressions have been misunderstood by commentators: *shub* "to turn one's attention to" (Ps. 85:9; 119:79; Isa. 31:6); *yadaᶜ* hiph. "to teach, instruct" (Isa. 40:13f.; Job 32:7; Prov. 9:9; 22:19, 21); *nabaᶜ* hiph. "to say" (literally, to pour out), cf. Ps. 19:3; 78:2; Prov. 15:28; etc. Two terms are used in a double sense: our "admonition" tries to capture both "reproof" and "instruction" (Prov. 5:12; 10:17) for *tokaḥat;* "mind" renders *ruaḥ,* which means both "anger" and "spirit" (in the sense of the best a teacher has to offer, Sir. 16:25).
8. The two expressions *tm'nw* (vs. 24) and *'bytm* (vs. 25) imply *lshmᶜ,* cf. 1 Sam. 8:19; Isa. 30:9.
9. The proper translation of *gam* is "really, emphatically," as in Judg. 8:9; Num. 24:12. Cf. Labuschagne 1966.
10. Cf. Isa. 5:25; Ezek. 6:14; Job 15:25; Humbert 1962:390ff.
11. Dalman 1928:202.
12. Cf. Prov. 3:25; Isa. 47:11.
13. Cf. Job 30:1; 31:29; Prov. 52:8. Cf. also Plato, *Republic* 613d.
14. Luke 14:28f.
15. Neumann 1971:9–37.
16. Bergson 1956:187.
17. Deut. 25:5–10, rsv.
18. Borger 1956:103f.
19. Judg. 10:12f.; Ezek. 8:18; 2 Chron. 36:15ff.
20. For the assumption that the original text spoke of the "fear of the gods," see ch. 11.
21. Cf. Prov. 13:2; 18:20f.; Isa. 3:10; Mic. 7:13.
22. See Prov. 1:19, rsv.
23. Cf. Prov. 1:10–15; 3:27–31.
24. Cf. Prov. 1:8f.; 1:17–19.
25. Sir. 38:24ff.

CHAPTER 6. *The Poem Proverbs 8:1–36*
1. Read the *qere.*
2. Read, with BHS, *nesakkoti.*
3. Read, with BHS, *beᶜazzezo.*
4. Read the *kethib.*

CHAPTER 7. *Two Kinds of Rhetoric: Didactic and Divine*
  1. Prov. 16:16; 3:14f. Cf. also Prov. 20:15; Job 22:24f; Ps. 19:11. According to Bryce 1979 (index sv. comparative proverb) this kind of saying originated in Egypt.
  2. Prov. 4:7; 17:16.
  3. Prov. 7:24. In Prov. 5:7 the same phrase marks the transition to the main section of a didactic discourse.
  4. Cf. Dion 1967.
  5. The assertion of Kayatz 1966:92 that "the more or less fixed structural pattern of Egyptian divine speech can be discerned in the Wisdom-speech of Prov. 8 as well" is exaggerated. In fact, the structural pattern she delineates does not exist at all, and the "challenge to listen" followed by an address is actually found, not in divine speeches, but in Egyptian royal inscriptions (ANET 231a, 233a, etc.). Nothing more than a general affinity of self-presentation, self-predication, etc. between the Egyptian divine speeches and Prov. 8 can be detected.
  6. Castellino 1972:57.
  7. Luckenbill 2:80.
  8. Luckenbill 2:226.

CHAPTER 8. *Wisdom: Patroness of Kings and Witness of Creation*
  1. Frankfort 1948:239.
  2. Ebeling 1955:181.
  3. Allam 1963:47 (temple at Denderah); Bergman 1968:169f. (temple at Philae).
  4. Keel 1978: nos. 262, 350; Winter 1983:245ff.
  5. For reciprocal love of king and deities in Egypt, see Morenz 1975:120–38. Corresponding biblical texts are more general and do not specifically involve kings, cf. Deut. 5:10 (= Exod. 20:6); 1 Sam. 2:30; 2 Chron. 15:2 (in negative terms: 2 Chron. 24:20; Zech. 7:13).
  6. Wisd. 6:3.
  7. Kloppenborg 1982:78.
  8. Ps. 104:2ff.; 65:7; 89:10f.; Isa. 51:9f.; Jer. 33:2; Zech. 12:2.
  9. Note the building terms *kwn* hiph. and *'mṣ* pi. "to build" Prov. 8:27–28; 2 Chron. 24:13; 35:20; and *ḥqq* "to draw (a plan)" Prov. 8:27; Ezek. 4:1.
  10. There are two possible interpretations of *ḥwg* in verse 27: the horizon, i.e., the line between the dome of heaven and the sea that surrounds the earth, *or* the dome affixed

163

over that horizon. Whereas Yee 1982:64, n. 21, opts for the second possibility, I prefer the first.

11. Gilbert 1979:209f.; Vawter 1980.
12. For this meaning of *qnh* cf. Deut. 32:6.
13. Niph. of *skk/škk* "to weave"; cf. similar contexts in Ps. 2:6; 139:13; Job 10:11.
14. Jer. 27:5; cf. Lang 1983a:49 and 1983b.
15. That the original El was later replaced by Yahweh was first suggested by Albright 1955:7.
16. Gen. 14:19.
17. In Ugaritic, *um ilm* and *qnyt ilm.*
18. Coffin Texts, spell 81 (Faulkner 1973:87).
19. "Your decree, El, is wise, your wisdom is everlasting . . . you are great, El, you are indeed wise" (Gibson 1977:60; cf. ANET 133). Cf. Caquot 1978. Cazelles 1969:31 defines El's wisdom as his "power of life and fertility."
20. Here are those who support the translations: (1) classical Jewish exegesis (Rüger 1977), NEB, Gilbert 1979:214, Plöger 1984; (2) Targum, McKane 1970, JPS; (3) Septuagint, Oesterley 1929 (cf. Akkadian *ummanu* "craftsman"), NAB, Passioni dell'Acqua 1984:128f; (4) McKane 1970 (another meaning of Akkadian *ummanu*); (5) Keel 1974:24f.; Bonnard 1979:119–23 (*'amon* is an apposition following a pronominal suffix).
21. Jer. 52:12; cf. A. Jepsen in a note on 2 Kings 25:11 in BHS.
22. In Zech. 8:5; Isa. 11:8 *šḥq* pi. and *shᶜᶜ* pilp. designate the playing of children. The terms *shᶜshwᶜym* and *shᶜᶜ* pilp. are also used for playing with young children: Isa. 66:12; Jer. 31:20.
23. In Egyptian *šd.tj nswt* "king's ward" and *hrdw n k3p* "child of the hiding place" (i.e., the children's quarter in the palace). Cf. Brunner 1957:12, 23 and the relevant entries in Erman/Grapow's *Wörterbuch,* vol. 4:377, 12 and 5:105, 11.
24. *Kalevala* 3:215–54, no doubt influenced by Job 15:7; 38:4.
25. 11QPsᵃCreat 4–7 (Sanders 1965:90).
26. Alt in Crenshaw 1976:102–12.
27. Gardiner 1947:2.
28. Wildeboer 1897:27.
29. Job 32:6ff.

1. *hl'* means "behold" as in 2 Kings 15:36; Job 22:12 (and often), and can remain untranslated.
2. For this meaning of *marom* cf. Jer. 51:53.
3. Sartre 1948:87: "L'écrivain s'adresse en principe à *tous* les hommes."
4. Ps. 117:1.
5. *ngydym* is a short form for *ngydym dbrym*, cf. Prov. 24:26; 2 Sam. 15:3. The same is true of *nkhym* and *yshrym* in verse 9.
6. Prov. 1:4.
7. Prov. 1:5.
8. "To inhabit shrewdness" (*shkn* followed by a place as in Isa. 33:5; Ps. 37:3; 135:21) seems to mean "to be shrewd." Given this odd expression one could also argue that "I am Wisdom" can actually mean "I am wise," like "I am prayer" = "I pray" Ps. 109:4, and "I am insight" = "I have insight" Prov. 8:14. Cf. Keel 1974:69.
9. Skehan 1979:368f.; Gilbert 1979:206.
10. McKane 1983:67.
11. McKane 1983:67.
12. Cf. Isa. 36:5 with Isa. 28:6; Judg. 8:21.
13. Divine wisdom: Job 12:13; divine hatred of evil: Ps. 5:6; Isa. 61:8; divine power: Job 12:13, 16;—royal wisdom: Isa. 11:2; royal hatred of evil: Ps. 45:8; royal power: Isa. 11:2.
14. 1 Sam. 16:18; Dan 2:23; 1:4.
15. Caquot 1978:27.
16. Weber 1947:341.
17. *cwshr wkbwd* is a hendiadys like *mhrws wmpz* in verse 19a.
18. For student and knowledge, cf. Prov. 2:4; 4:6; 7:4; for man and woman, Prov. 18:22; 31:10; Cant 3:1f.; for God and human individuals, Deut. 6:5; Hos. 5:6; Jer. 29:13.
19. Thus in 1 Kings 5:1 Hiram king of Tyre is reported to have always *loved* David. Cf. Moran 1963.
20. Schmid 1968.
21. Faulkner 1937:172.
22. Pliny, *Natural History* 7:72.
23. Keel 1974:68 on the basis of Gen. 21:8ff.
24. Keel 1974:69f.
25. Job 38:f. Cf. 11QPsaCreat 5 (Sanders 1965:90). The interpretation was suggested by a rabbi of the second century

A.D., see Aboth de R. Nathan A 31 (Schechter 1887:46a) and is implied in Milton's *Paradise Lost* 7:7–12. Milton invokes his heavenly muse who, with Wisdom her sister, played "in the presence of the almighty Father, pleased with thy celestial song."

26. *hkm* can take on an "ingressive" meaning, cf. Prov. 19:20; 23:19.

27. A short expression for '*l tprᶜw mwsr,* "do not spurn instruction," cf. Prov. 1:25; 13:18; 15:32.

28. For *mṣ'* "to acquire, attain" cf. Prov. 8:9 and Ceresco 1982.

29. "Happy is/are . . . ," cf. Prov. 3:13; 14:21.

30. Prov. 3:21f.; 4:1f., 20.

31. Prov. 1:22; 5:12f.; 9:8.

32. Prov. 3:13; cf. 4:22.

33. The house is only referred to by implication; it is represented by "door(s)" and "threshold" in verse 34.

34. Sir. 51:23, dating from around 200 B.C. It is unclear whether 2 Kings 6:1–7 refers to a residential structure for students or to an actual school building. For students meeting their teacher in the latter's home, cf. Gevaryahu 1983.

35. Sir. 6:36. The Hebrew term used, *shhr* pi. "to seek" reminds of *shhr* "dawn."

36. Talmud, bShabbath 127a.

37. This seems to be true also for Prov. 12:2; 18:22, where the same expression is used.

38. Prov. 3:4. Expressions like "favor in the eyes of gods and men" are current in ancient sources, cf. van der Weiden 1970:30, 37f.; Lang 1972:75.

CHAPTER 11. *A Textual Intrusion: Proverbs 9:7–10*

1. "Fear of Yahweh" mottoes can be found in the introduction of another two wisdom writings: Prov. 22:19; Sir. 1:11f. In Ps. 111:10 and Job 28:28 a similar aphorism is placed at the end of poems.

2. Prov. 1:1–7 is encompassed by *hkmh wmwsr* in verses 2a and 7b. To assume that verse 7 is purely secondary is thus unlikely, cf. Avishur 1984:237f.

3. That Prov. 9:10 must be a restyled older motto was first suggested by Pope 1955:14. For him, it "is to be regarded as a clumsy modification of the older Canaanite formula in which El stood in parallelism with *qedoshim.*" For a

166

stylistic analysis of verse 10b that involves two synonyms (*dᶜt, bynh*), cf. Avishur 1984:254.
4. von Rad 1976:181 on *yir'at 'elohim* in Gen. 20:11.
5. Deut. 33:2; Job 5:1; 15:15; Ps. 89:6ff. "Holy ones" is a standard epithet for the council of gods in Phoenician inscriptions (Lindenberger 1983:70).
6. Haran 1982.
7. Other reconstructions of the perplexing textual history have been proposed by Scott 1965 and Goldingay 1977. Scott takes Prov. 9:1–6, 10–12 as the original text, whereas Goldingay finds it in Prov. 9:1–6, 11. These suggestions are attractive because they provide an easy solution to the problem why Folly, as a simple city harlot (see ch. 13), can be a goddess's rival. The added lines on Folly would assume that Wisdom, too, is just a playful personification.

CHAPTER 12. *Invitation to a Banquet in a House of Seven Pillars*
1. See, for instance, Ahlström 1979.
2. E. Stern in Mazar 1979:269. Cf. Beebe 1968:50ff.
3. Yadin 1975:152.
4. Yadin 1975:170f.; Fritz 1980:122ff. (house no. 167).
5. Ismail 1975:38f.
6. Lewis 1976:175.
7. 1 Kings 8:62f.; 2 Chron. 7:4f.; 30:24. For Assyria cf. Renger 1970.
8. ANET 558–60.
9. Deut. 20:5.
10. Westermarck 1920:65.
11. *Enuma elish* 6:45–60 (ANET 68f.).
12. Gibson 1977:63f.
13. Borger 1956:116.
14. ANET 125f.
15. Gibson 1977:93.
16. Job 34:3.
17. Sir. 51:24; 15:3.
18. Isa. 55:1–3. Cf. Lindblom 1925:122.

CHAPTER 13. *Folly—a Harlot*
1. 1 Kings 15:12; 2 Kings 23:7.
2. Isa. 57:5ff.; Hos. 3:13f.
3. Greeley 1977:76.

4. The problem of "sacred prostitution" is discussed by Arnaud 1973, Conzelmann 1974, Fisher 1976, Winter 1983:334–42, Barstad 1984:22–33. Cf. also what Kraus 1974:243–46 says about the "sacred marriage" ritual sometimes confused with "sacred prostitution."

5. Said 1979:190.

6. Matt. 1:5; Gen. 38.

7. Niditch 1979:147.

8. Amos 7:17.

9. 2 Kings 23:7.

10. Gen. 38:14; Josh. 2 (with the "scarlet cloth" hanging in Rahab's window as sign of her trade?).

11. Wiseman 1964; Schneider 1913:1341.

12. Mansi 13:756.

13. CAD H 101b (with reference to goddess Ishtar who assumes the role of a harlot).

14. Plautus, *Poenulus* 266.

15. For Greek musicians/prostitutes cf. Schneider 1913: 1341f., 1349f.

16. It may be, however, that the prophet refers to cultic structures he denounces as brothel-like.

17. Cf. Akkadian *ram* "to settle down" and Ugaritic *rmm* "to erect a building."

18. Xenophon, *Memorabilia of Socrates* 2:1, 23f. (ET, E. C. Marchant 1923). Confronting two persons, ideas, points of view, or the like was a common device of ancient rhetoric and is called *synkrisis* or *comparatio* (Lausberg 1960: §799, 1130). For echoes of "Hercules at the Crossroads" and Prov. 9, cf. Goethe's *Wilhelm Meisters Lehrjahre* 1:8 and G. K. Chesterton's poem "The Two Women."

19. Lang 1972:87–91. The symbolic character of the adulteress is particularly evident in the Septuagint.

20. 4Q 184, a text known as "The Wiles of the Wicked Woman" (Allegro 1964); Stammler 1959.

21. Boström 1935, now followed by Perdue 1977:146–55, understands Lady Folly as representing the Canaanite goddess of love who invites Israelite men to her home in order to celebrate some orgiastic ritual. What here the goddess does herself would normally have been done by nonorthodox Israelite women who practiced an orgiastic ritual in their homes. For the ritual they needed a man to

whom they were not married. This construction is based on a daring extrapolation from Proverbs 7: a woman invites someone during the absence of her husband to share both her bed and what are probably the leftovers of a sacrificial meal she took home from the temple. Boström also refers to Herodotus. According to Herodotus 1:199 or his doubtful informants, every Babylonian woman had to give herself to a foreigner outside the Aphrodite sanctuary in which she had to wait for a patron. For recent assessments of the Herodotus passage, see Conzelmann 1974:162–66, Arnaud 1973, Winter 1983:335ff.

CHAPTER 14. *Brief Commentary on Proverbs 9:1–6, 11–18*

1. "She calls" is the literal translation; the context of verse 2 suggests that she calls through the mouth of her maids.

2. Literally, "on the towers *(gpy)* of the city walls," "on top of *(ᶜl gpy)* the city walls," (HAL 192b) or, understood as a synonymous hendiadys in the sense of Avishur 1984, simply "on the city walls."

3. *ḥsr-lb* is a *casus pendens,* placed at the beginning and resumed by *lw.*

4. For *nśʾ* "to bear (consequences)" cf. Job 34:31.

5. Prov. 1:20f.; 8:2a.

6. Prov. 4:11.

7. Cf. Prov. 3:2; 7:2a; Lang 1972:66–69.

8. Cf. Prov. 1:4.

9. Cf. Prov. 7:7; 9:16; 10:13; Wolff 1973:80–84.

10. Literally, "her house," "her seven pillars," etc. with a redundant pronoun, cf. Blau 1979.

11. For *ḥsb ᶜmwdym* cf. ch. 1, note 5.

12. For *ʾp* "and" cf. Dahood 1970:399.

13. Talmud, b. Sanh. 38a. According to this text, Wisdom is God, the palace is the world, and the guests invited are Adam and Eve.

14. Job 1:4; Ezek. 23:40; Luke 14:17; Matt. 22:3.

15. Gen. 24:61; 1 Sam. 25:42; Exod. 2:5; Esth. 2:9; cf. Ps. 45:15; Prov. 31:15; Cant. 6:8.

16. Dahood 1963:16f. This commentator suggested that the maids were not actually sent out as messengers, but simply "dismissed" (Heb. *shalaḥ*) after they had prepared the meal. This is implausible in view of the standard phrase "to send out a messenger *(shalaḥ)* in order to invite *(qaraʾ)*

169

someone," cf. Gen. 27:42; Num. 22:37; Josh. 24:9; etc.

17. Burder 1840:330.
18. ANET 519.
19. Matt. 22:4. For ancient parallels cf. Homer, *Odyssey* 3:436–73; Gibson 1977:58, 63f.; Lichtenstein 1968/69: 24–29; Edmunds 1982.
20. Gordon 1965:148.
21. Robert Lowth on Isa. 1:22, quoted by Freeman 1972:235f. Outside of the poem, Israelite teachers discourage the drinking of mixed (spiced) wine: Prov. 23:30; Isa. 5:22. Cf. Brown 1969: 153–55; Vogt 1967:69–72.
22. Tristram 1894:82. Cf. Luke 14:16f., Fernea 1969:87, 96f. The same rule applies to both formal and informal invitations.
23. ANET 75b.
24. Cf. Said 1979:186: "*Alemah* in Arabic means a learned woman. It was the name given to women in conservative eighteenth-century Egyptian society who were accomplished reciters of poetry. By the mid-nineteenth century the title was used as a sort of guild name for dancers who were also prostitutes."
25. Loretz 1982:147 emphasizes that these are not just "shades" as the common translations suggest.
26. Cf. Prov. 4:19; 7:23; Job. 36:12; Isa. 47:11.
27. Prov. 5:5.
28. Prov. 23:27.
29. Prov. 2:18; 7:27.
30. Prov. 7:22f.
31. *'sht ksylwt* means "foolish woman"; cf. *'sht ḥyl* (Prov. 31:10) "capable woman."
32. Tentative translation of *hwmyh* (JPS). The word refers to restless and noisy behavior, cf. Prov. 7:11; Gerleman 1973.
33. *ptywt* "(craft of) seduction" (cf. Exod. 22:15) is in *casus pendens;* for *wbl ydᶜh mh* cf. 2 Sam. 18:29.
34. Tentative rendering of, literally, "on a chair, the city wall."
35. Josh. 2:15.
36. Talmud, b. Nid. 16b.
37. Josh. 2:18.
38. In Prov. 7:10 *nṣwrt lb* seems to mean "tightly laced

170

bosom"; for *lb* "bosom" cf. Nah. 2:8. Cf. the colorful breastband of Aphrodite in the *Iliad* 14:214–23.
39. Cf. Gen. 38:14ff.
40. Ezek. 16:25.
41. Cf. Prov. 15:21.
42. For "eating" and "drinking" as sexual metaphors cf. Prov. 5:15; 30:20; Cant. 5:1; Sir. 23:17. In 1 Tim 4:3, RSV, those who "enjoin abstinence from foods which God created" seem to encourage celibate life. For "stealing" as metaphor for illicit sexual relations cf. "thief" for an adulterer (Jer. 2:26; Ps. 50:18) and, in Akkadian, "female thief" *(sharraqitum)* for a harlot (CAD H 101a).

CHAPTER 15. *Mysterious Wisdom*
1. View (a) is that of Albright (1946:283f.) and Wilckens (1964:508f.); (b) is advocated by Donner (1957:10); (c), by commentators Gemser (1963:23, 49) and Plöger (1984:98, 111), who speak of "poetic personification," as well as by von Rad (1970:205ff.), who identifies Wisdom as a personification of the cosmic order. See the discussion in ch. 18.

CHAPTER 16. *The Origin and Nature of Biblical Monotheism*
1. For this chapter see Smith 1971 and Lang 1983a:13–59.
2. 2 Kings 23:5.
3. Josh. 24; Judg. 6:25–32.
4. ANEP 355.
5. 2 Kings 18:4.
6. Cf. Lang 1983b.
7. Cf. Ezek. 37 with imagery taken from a Zoroastrian burial ground; Isa. 26:19.
8. In Hebrew inscriptions from Hirbet el-Qom and Kuntillet Ajrud, some scholars have found the name of Asherah, which they took to be Yahweh's spouse, but this seems to be an epigraphically incorrect reading. The purport of the goddess Anat-Yahu in papyri of the Jewish colony on the island of Elephantine in Egypt or her relationship to Yahweh is unknown. One scholar takes her to be Yahweh's daughter (Kraeling 1953:91); according to Porten (1968:171), she is rather his consort. Cf. Winter 1983:486–508; Dever 1984; Zevit 1984.
9. 1 Kings 22:19; Job 1:6.
10. Winnett 1938; Mooren 1981:555ff.
11. The worshiper of the Ugaritic god El is immediately

involved with the "sons of El" and Athirat, El's consort; see Beyerlin 1978:222.

12. Matt. 13:57.
13. van Selms 1973.
14. Hos. 13:4; Isa. 45:21.

CHAPTER 17. *Wisdom: A Hebrew Goddess Redefined*

1. Koch 1984:103.
2. Cf. Job 31:24–28.
3. Koch 1976:316.
4. Job 29:5f.
5. See Septuagint text of Gen. 17:1; 28:3; 35;11; etc.
6. Cf. his apologetical treatise *Kitāb al Fiṣal* (Asín Palacios 1928:367).
7. For Nisaba cf. Haussig 1965:115f.; Sjöberg 1976:174f.; for Seshat cf. Bonnet 1952:699.—Scholars are now increasingly becoming aware of the originally divine nature of Lady Wisdom, although the futile search for an immediate extra-Israelite "model," allegedly "copied" in Israel, is still very much on their mind, see Winter 1983:511–14. Winter and others consider the Egyptian goddess Maat to be this model (without being able to produce convincing evidence). There is, however, evidence for the Hellenistic goddess Isis to be the book of Wisdom's model for Wisdom *(Sophia),* cf. Kloppenborg 1982.
8. Gen. 14:19.
9. Cf. Ch. 11.
10. The text in question reads: "From heaven the peoples are favoured; Wisdom is of the gods. Indeed, she is precious to the gods; her kingdom is eternal. She has been established by Shamayn (?); yes, the Holy Lord has exalted her" (Lindenberger 1983:68). The Assyrian provenance of the Ahiqar novel is clear from the reference made to seventh-century Assyrian kings Sanherib and Esarhaddon as well as to the Assyrian god Shamash. The exaltation of a deity, that is, his or her promotion to a higher rank, is a feature the Ahiqar passage shares with Mesopotamian mythology. Thus the goddess Inanna is boasting in a hymn that she has received lordship over heaven, earth, ocean, and war, for the god Enlil has "exalted" her (ANET 578f.). Cf. Hallo/van Dijk 1968; Hrushka 1969. According to Lindenberger 1983:68, Wisdom, in the

Ahiqar passage, would be "the special province of Baal Shamayn, one of the high gods of the Aramaeans"; the reading Shamayn, however, is conjectural. Lindenberger suggests north Syria as the home of Ahiqar.

11. Friedrich Schiller, "The Gods of Greece," poem; translated in Boening 1977:377.

12. A notable exception is Camp 1985:ch. 7.

13. Pötscher 1972.

14. Cicero, *On the Nature of the Gods* 2:61: *Omnium rerum quia vis erat tanta, ut sine deo regi non posset, ipsa res deorum nomen obtinuit.*

15. Zech. 2:14; Isa. 52:9; Ps. 96:11ff.; 85:10; 89:14; Gal. 3:24. Cf. Gerleman 1966.

16. Isa. 47:1ff.

17. Isa. 51:17–23.

18. Zech. 11:1–5.

19. Fitzgerald 1972:416 feels that the city goddess concept was pagan and "that the canonical Hebrew poet-theologians adopt this Canaanite point of view for purely literary purposes."

20. Preminger 1975:612.

21. Guglielmi 1972:984. The text is in Lichtheim 2:211–14.

22. Mattingly 1960:66. While the artists of revolutionary France gave Liberty the round cap of the freed slave as an emblem, Bartholdi has her hold the torch of enlightenment.

23. Mattingly 1937.

24. Mattingly 1928/29:164f.

25. The personification category was used by commentators Hadrianus (PG 98:1285f.) and Mercerus (1573). According to John Milton, the Wisdom of Proverbs 8 "is not the Son of God who is there introduced as the speaker, but a poetical personification of wisdom, as in Job 28:20–27" (Milton 1933:13). There is evidence for a similar view in the poetical work of the Nuremberg *Meistersinger* Hans Sachs (Sachs 1870:238ff.).

CHAPTER 18. *Hypostasis—Wisdom Myth—the Voice of Creation*

1. On divergent uses on the concept of hypostasis, cf. Rodriguez-Herranz 1972:56–60. Some confusion has been caused by the definition of Bousset/Gressmann 1926:342f.: "Like angels, hypostases are intermediate beings between God and the world who enable Him to

173

do His work in the world . . . strange dual beings." Since, according to this description, beings that are not subject-identical with the divinity do not belong to the category of hypostasis, Goldberg 1969:535f. has refused to apply it to the Jewish *Shekinah.*

2. Pfeifer 1967:68–76. For the "messenger of Yahweh" figure, see Röttger 1978.
3. Johnson 1961:13–22, 28–37.
4. Donner 1957:10; Whybray 1965:92–104.
5. Weber 1897:177. Cf. Schencke 1913:2–7.
6. Schencke 1913:7; Bousset/Gressmann 1926:342–54.
7. Schencke 1913:82–86; Rankin 1936:342–54.
8. Ringgren 1947:129ff. has demonstrated that there is no model for Wisdom among the Persian hypostases. For these cf. Boyce 1975:192–228.
9. Schechter 1961:21–24.
10. Pfeifer 1967:53–57; Mack 1973:179–84.
11. "The poem Prov. 8:22–31," explains Whybray (1965:103), "is no more than an expansion, in personified terms, of the statement in 3:19 that 'Yahweh founded the earth *by* wisdom.' "
12. This seems to be Gilbert's (1979:215, 217) view.
13. Larcher 1969:409.
14. Albright 1919/20:285ff.; Bultmann (1923) 1967; Wilckens 1959:160–97 and 1964:508f.
15. Wilckens 1959:165.
16. Wilckens 1959:174f.
17. Gemser 1963:48f. and Christ 1970:49 insist on differentiating between Proverbs 1—9 and Gnostic mythology.
18. After Charlesworth 1:33.
19. Cf. Hos. 6:3.
20. Cf. Jer. 5:1f.; Ps. 55:12.
21. Hesiod, *Works and Days* 197–209; Theognis, *Elegies* 1135–42; Aratos, *Constellations* 100–35. Cf. Bergmeier 1981.
22. Aratos, *Constellations* 133–35.
23. Wilckens 1964:509.
24. von Rad 1972:144. The quotations that follow are from this work.
25. Sir. 1:9.
26. Job 12:7ff.; Ps. 97:6.
27. Gibson 1977:49 (ANET 136). The translator of the Ugaritic text compares Ps. 19:2–5; 42:8; Hos. 2:23f.

CHAPTER 19. *Lady Wisdom in Church, Speculation, and Mysticism*

1. Judg. 16.
2. 2 Sam. 15:25.
3. 1 Sam. 10:23; 2 Kings 2:23.
4. Homer, *Iliad* 2:217ff.
5. Diogenes Laertius 5:1; 7:1.
6. Tacitus, *Agricola* 44.
7. Matt. 7:20; Num. 13:23ff.
8. Chadwick 1932:404–07; Boman 1968:60ff. For further insight cf. the celebrated first ch. of Auerbach's *Mimesis* (1953:1ff.) and Iser (1978) on "indeterminacy" in literature.
9. Hennecke 2:243. Cf von Dobschütz 1928:1ff. There is no description of what Jesus looked like before the sixth century A.D.: von Dobschütz 1899, appendix 295ff.
10. Heller 1984:3 developing 1 Kings 1:4.
11. Jacobsen 1929. Regarding iconography, cf., in general, Mielke 1972, Schiller 1976:68–77.
12. Schott 1950:39; ANET 144 (lines 143ff.); Jax 1933:6, 40, 61f.
13. Claudel 21:350.
14. Quoted in Nigg 1972:210f.
15. Prov. 4:8.
16. The oldest evidence is Sir. 24:23; cf. also Bar 4:4; 11QPsa 154:12–14 (Sanders 1965:65). Cf. Hengel 1973:307–18; Marböck 1976; Küchler 1979:31–61, 102–05; Nickelsburg/Stone 1983:203–31 (anthology of early Jewish texts on Wisdom).
17. For recent assessments of the evidence see Christ 1970; van Roon 1974; Wilken 1975:1–66; Bonnard 1979: 135–49; Schüssler Fiorenza 1983:130–35, 188–92.
18. 'Abot R. Nat. A 31 (Schechter 1887:46a).
19. Tg. Yer. II and Tg. Neof. I to Gen. 1:1. In the New Testament: John 1:1–3; 1 Cor. 8:6; Col. 1:15f.; Heb. 1:2; cf. Hengel 1973:110; Zeilinger 1974. In Col. 1, Christ is not the creator of the world, but of the *new* world: Aurrecoechea 1974.
20. This is Suggs' (1970:15) reconstruction of the original Q passage.
21. Luke 11:49–51; Matt. 23:34–36.
22. Justin, *Dialogue* 61 (PG 6:613–16); Hippolyt (PG 10:621f.,

625f.); Origen (PG 13:27f.; 17:185f.).

23. Irenaeus, *Against Heresies* 4:20, 3; Nigg 1972:217.
24. Kern 1971:83.
25. Pseudo-Athanasius (PG 26:292f.); the pietistic *Berlenburg Bible* to Prov. 8; Solovyev (cf. Pfleger 1964:86f.); Frank-Duquesne 1955:156, 238.
26. Claudel 13:219–43.
27. First in Paterius (PL 79:901). Cf. also Moore 1927:250.
28. MacRae 1970; Rudolph 1980.
29. Thus the fourth-century *Apocryphon of John,* cf. Leipoldt/Grundmann 1967:348–87.
30. Leipoldt/Grundmann 1967:380.
31. Thus the system of Valentinos (second century A.D.), cf. Leipoldt/Grundmann 1967:392–95.
32. Augustine, *Treatise on the Gospel of John* 1:61f.; Staudenmaier 1840:30–42; Ott 1965:97.
33. *Der Prediger und Katechet* 113 (1974) 487.
34. Gelin 1954:89.
35. Wisd. 8:2ff.; Horsley 1979.
36. Dölger 1950.
37. Seuse 1966:24f.
38. Bremond 6:93–96.
39. Cioran 1977; Boulgakov 1983; von Lilienfeld 1984.
40. Teilhard de Chardin 1968:192. An echo of this poem can be seen in texts by Pierre Emmanuel (1973:348, 410f., 415).

SOURCES OF ILLUSTRATIONS

Figure 1. Tufnell 1953:118, fig. 10. Reproduced by permission of the Wellcome Institute, London.

Figure 2. After Aharoni 1982:210, fig. 66.

Figure 3. Engraving after an ancient fresco, now in the Museum of Naples, Italy. Bonner 1977:118, fig. 11.

Figure 4. Landauer 1925:no. 191 (Bruno Hentschel Kunstverlag, Leipzig).

Figure 5. The fragmentary Babylonian clay tablet, here reproduced without the text written on it, is in the British Museum; Keel 1978, fig. 8. Reproduced by permission of Benziger Verlag, Zurich.

Figure 6. Shilo 1973:280, fig. 4. (The actual remains are described by Yadin 1975:152f.) Reproduced by permission of The Israel Exploration Society, Jerusalem.

Figure 7. Fritz 1980:125, fig. 3 (house no. 167). Reproduced by permission of Otto Harrassowitz Verlag, Wiesbaden.

Figure 8. Lane 1954:385.

Figure 9. New Kingdom relief from Thebes, Egypt. Brunner-Traut 1976:70, fig. 19. Reproduced by permission of Kohlhammer Verlag, Stuttgart.

BIBLIOGRAPHY

Aharoni, Yohanan. "Tel Beersheva." *RB* 80(1973)405–08.
———. *The Archaeology of the Land of Israel.* London: SCM Press, 1982.
Ahlström, Gösta W. "The House of Wisdom." *SEÅ* 44(1979)74–76.
Albright, William F. "The Goddess of Life and Wisdom." *AJSL* 36(1919/20)258–94.
———. *From the Stone Age to Christianity,* 2d ed. Baltimore: Johns Hopkins University Press, 1946.
———. "Some Canaanite-Phoenician Sources of Hebrew Wisdom." *VTS* 3 (1955)1–15.
Aletti, Jean-Noël. "Proverbes 8, 22–31: Etude de structure." *Biblica* 57(1976)25–37.
Allam, Schafik. *Beiträge zum Hathorkult.* Berlin: Deutscher Kunstverlag, 1963.
Allegro, John M. "The Wiles of the Wicked Woman." *PEQ* 96(1964)53–55.
Arnaud, Daniel. "La prostitution sacrée en Mésopotamie, un mythe historiographique?" *RHR* 183(1973)111–15.
Arzt, M. "The Teacher in Talmud and Midrash." In *Mordecai M. Kaplan Jubilee Volume.* New York: Jewish Theological Seminary, 1953, 35–47.
Asín Palacios, Miguel. *Abenházam de Córdoba y su Historia crítica de las ideas religiosas,* vol. 2. Madrid: Real Academia de la Historia, 1928.
Auerbach, Erich. *Mimesis.* ET, W. R. Trask. Princeton: Princeton University Press, 1953.
Aurrecoechea, J. L. "Los títulos cristológicos de Colosenes 1,15–16." *Estudios Trinitarios* 8(1974)307–28.
Avishur, Yitzhak. *Stylistic Studies of Word-Pairs in Biblical and Ancient*

Semitic Literatures. AOAT 210. Kevelaer: Butzon & Bercker, 1984.

Barr, James. *Old and New in Interpretation.* London: SCM Press, 1966.

Barstad, Hans M. *The Religious Polemics of Amos.* VTS 34. Leiden: Brill, 1984.

Beebe, H. Keith. "Ancient Palestinian Dwellings." *BA* 31(1968)38–58.

Bergman, Jan. *Ich bin Isis.* Acta Univ. Upsaliensis: Historia Religionum 3. Uppsala, Sweden: Almqvist & Wiksell, 1968.

Bergmeier, Roland. "Weisheit—Dike—Lichtjungfrau." *Journal for the Study of Judaism* 12(1981)75–86.

Bergson, Henri. "Laughter." In *Comedy*, edited by Wylie Sypher. Garden City, NY: Doubleday, 1956, 59–190.

[Berlenburg Bible] *Die Heilige Schrift und zwar Alten Testaments*, Dritter Teil. Berlenburg, 1730.

Beyerlin, Walter, ed. *Near Eastern Religious Texts Relating to the Old Testament.* Philadelphia: Westminster Press, 1978.

Blau, Joshua. "Redundant Pronominal Suffixes Denoting Intrinsic Possession." *JANES* 11(1979)31–37.

Boening, John, ed. *The Reception of Classical German Literature in England, 1760–1860*, vol. 10. New York: Garland, 1977.

Bollnow, Otto Friedrich. *Wesen und Wandel der Tugenden.* Frankfurt: Ullstein, 1958.

Boman, Thorleif. *Das hebräische Denken im Vergleich mit dem griechischen*, 5th ed. Göttingen: Vandenhoeck & Ruprecht, 1968.

Bonnard, P.-E. "De la Sagesse personnifiée dans l'Ancien Testament à la Sagesse en personne dans le Nouveau." In *La Sagesse de l'Ancien Testament*, edited by M. Gilbert. Leuven: University Press, 1979, 117–49.

Bonner, Stanley F. "The Street-Teacher." *American Journal of Philology* 93(1973)509–29.

———. *Education in Ancient Rome.* Berkeley: University of California Press, 1977.

Bonnet, Hans. *Reallexikon der ägyptischen Religionsgeschichte.* Berlin: de Gruyter, 1952.

Borger, Rykle. *Die Inschriften Asarhaddons Königs von Assyrien.* Graz: Selbstverlag E. Weidner, 1956.

Boström, Gustav. *Proverbiastudien: Die Weisheit und das fremde Weib in Spr 1–9.* Lunds Universitets Årsskrift N.F. Avd. 1, vol. 30:3. Lund: C. W. K. Gleerup, 1935.

Boulgakov, Serge. *La Sagesse de Dieu*, ET, C. Andronikoff. Lausanne: L'Age d'homme, 1983.

Bousset, Wilhelm, and Gressmann, Hugo. *Die Religion des Judentums im späthellenistischen Zeitalter.* Tübingen: J. C. B. Mohr, 1926.

Boyce, Mary. *A History of Zoroastrianism,* vol. 1. Leiden: Brill, 1975.

Bremond, Henri. *Histoire littéraire du sentiment religieux en France,* vol. 6. Paris: Bloud & Gay, 1923.

Brown, John P. "The Mediterranean Vocabulary of the Vine." *VT* 19(1969)146–70.

Brunner, Hellmut. *Altägyptische Erziehung.* Wiesbaden: Harrassowitz, 1957.

Brunner-Traut, Emma. *Die Alten Ägypter,* 2d ed. Stuttgart: Kohlhammer, 1976.

Bryce, Glendon E. *A Legacy of Wisdom: The Egyptian Contribution to the Wisdom of Israel.* Lewisburg, PA: Bucknell University Press, 1979.

Bultmann, Rudolf. "Der religionsgeschichtliche Hintergrund des Prologs zum Johannes-Evangelium." In *Exegetica.* Tübingen: J. C. B. Mohr, 1967, 10–35.

Burder, Samuel. *Oriental Customs; or an Illustration of the Sacred Scriptures,* new ed. by W. Groser. London: Th. Tegg, 1840.

Burford, Alison. *Craftsmen in Greek and Roman Society.* London: Thames & Hudson, 1972.

Camp, Claudia. *Wisdom and the Feminine in the Book of Proverbs.* Decatur, GA: Almond Press, 1985.

Caquot, André. "Israelite Perceptions of Wisdom and Strength in the Light of the Ras Shamra Texts." In *Israelite Wisdom: Theological and Literary Essays in Honor of S. Terrien.* Missoula, MT: Scholars Press, 1978, 25–33.

Castellino, G. R. *Two Shulgi Hymns (BC).* Rome: Instituto di Studi del Vicino Oriente, 1972.

Cazelles, Henri. "Essai sur le pouvoir de la divinité en Ugarit et en Israel." *Ugaritica,* vol. 6. Paris: Geuthner, 1969, 25–44.

Ceresco, Anthony R. "The Function of Antanaclasis (mṣ' "to find"/mṣ', "to reach, overtake, grasp") in Hebrew Poetry." *CBQ* 44 (1982) 551–69.

Chadwick, Hector M., and Chadwick, N. K. *The Growth of Literature,* vol. 1. Cambridge: Cambridge University Press, 1932.

Charlesworth, James H., ed. *The Old Testament Pseudepigrapha,* vol. 1. London: Darton, Longman & Todd, 1983.

Chase, Mary Ellen. *The Bible and the Common Reader.* New York: Macmillan, 1944.

Christ, Felix. *Jesus-Sophia: Die Sophia-Christologie bei den Synoptikern.* Zürich: Zwingli-Verlag, 1970.

Cicero, Marcus Tullius. *On Oratory and Orators.* ET, J. S. Watson. Carbondale: Southern Illinois University Press, 1970.

Cioran, Samuel D. *Vladimir Solov'ev and the Knighthood of the Divine Sophia.* Waterloo, Ont.: Wilfried Laurier University Press, 1977.

Claudel, Paul. *Oeuvres complètes,* vols. 13 and 21. Paris: Gallimard, 1958 and 1963.

Conzelmann, Hans. "Korinth und die Mädchen der Aphrodite." In *Theologie als Schriftauslegung.* Munich: Kaiser, 1974, 152–66.

Crenshaw, James L., ed. *Studies in Ancient Israelite Wisdom.* New York: KTAV, 1976.

Cross, Frank M. "Prose and Poetry in the Mythic and Epic Texts from Ugarit." *HTR* 67(1974)1–15.

Dahood, Mitchell. *Proverbs and Northwest-Semitic Philology.* Rome: Biblical Institute Press, 1963.

———. *Psalms,* vol. 3. *The Anchor Bible.* Garden City, NY: Doubleday, 1970.

Daiches, S. "Note on the Word *ḥṣbh* in Proverbs ix.1." *Expository Times* 55(1943/44)277.

Dalman, Gustav. *Arbeit und Sitte in Palästina,* vol. 1:1. Gütersloh: Bertelsmann, 1928.

Dever, William G. "Asherah, Consort of Yahweh? New Evidence from Kuntillet ᶜAjrud." *BASOR* 255(1984)21–37.

Dimitrovsky, H. Z., ed. *Exploring the Talmud,* vol. 1. New York: KTAV, 1976.

Dion, H.-M. "Le genre littéraire sumérien de l'hymne à soi-même et quelques passages du Deutéro-Isaïe." *RB* 74(1967)194–234.

von Dobschütz, Ernst. *Christusbilder.* Texte und Untersuchungen 18. Leipzig: Hinrichs, 1899.

———. *Der Apostel Paulus,* vol. 2. Halle: Waisenhaus, 1928.

Dölger, Franz. "Christus als himmlischer Eros und Seelenbräutigam bei Origenes." *Antike und Christentum* 6(1950)273–75.

Donner, Herbert. "Die religionsgeschichtlichen Ursprünge von Prov. 8." *ZÄS* 82(1958)8–18.

Ebeling, Erich. "Beiträge zur Kenntnis des Beschwörungsserie Namburbi." *ZA* 49(1955)178–92.

Edmunds, Lowell. "The Latin Invitation Poem." *American Journal of Philology* 103(1982)184–88.

Eliot, T. S. *The Sacred Wood. Essays on Poetry and Criticism.* New York: Methuen, 1980.

Emmanuel, Pierre. *Sophia.* Paris: Seuil, 1973.

Erman, Adolf, and Grapow, Hermann. *Wörterbuch der ägyptischen*

182

Sprache, vols. 1–7, and *Belegstellen*, vols. 1–5. Berlin: Akademie-Verlag, 1940–63.

Evans, Geoffrey. "Gates and Streets: Urban Institutions in Old Testament Times." *Journal of Religious History* 2(1962/63)1–12.

Faulkner, R. O. *The Ancient Egyptian Coffin Texts*, vol. 1 Warminster: Aris & Phillips, 1973).

Fernea, Elizabeth F. *Guests of the Sheik. An Ethnography of an Iraqi Village.* Garden City, NY: Doubleday, 1969.

Fish, Stanley. *Is There a Text in This Class? The Authority of Interpretive Communities.* Cambridge, MA: Harvard University Press, 1980.

Fisher, Eugene J. "Cultic Prostitution in the Ancient Near East? A Reassessment." *Biblical Theology Bulletin* 6(1976)225–36.

Fitzgerald, Aloysius. "The Mythological Background for the Presentation of Jerusalem as a Queen." *CBQ* 34(1972)403–16.

Francke, W. K. "The Function of 'wis' in the Characterization of Gahmuret, Gawan and Parcival." *Modern Language Notes* 87(1972)409–18.

Frank-Duquesne, Albert. *Schöpfung und Zeugung: Philosophie und Mystik der Ehe.* Düsseldorf: Patmos, 1955.

Frankfort, Henri. *Kingship and the Gods: A Study of Ancient Near Eastern Religion.* Chicago: University of Chicago Press, 1948.

Freeman, James M. *Manners and Customs of the Bible.* Plainfield, NJ: Logos International, 1972.

Frick, Frank S. *The City in Ancient Israel.* Missoula, MT: Scholars Press, 1977.

Fritz, Volkmar. "Die kulturhistorische Bedeutung der früheisenzeitlichen Siedlung auf Hirbet el-Mshash und das Problem der Landnahme." *ZDPV* 96(1980)121–35.

Gardiner, Alan H. *Ancient Egyptian Onomastica*, vol. 1. London: Oxford University Press, 1947.

Gelin, A. "Le chant de l'infante." *Bible et vie chrétienne* 7(1954)89–95.

Gemser, Berend. *Sprüche Salomos*, 2d ed. Handbuch zum Alten Testament. Tübingen: J. C. B. Mohr, 1963.

Gerleman, Gillis. "Bemerkungen zum alttestamentlichen Sprachstil." In *Studia biblica et semitica T. C. Vriezen . . . dedicata.* Wageningen: Veenman & Zonen, 1966, 108–14.

————. "Die lärmende Menge: Der Sinn des hebräischen Wortes *hamon*." In *Wort und Geschichte. AOAT* 18. Neukirchen: Neukirchener Verlag, 1973, 71–75.

Gerstenberger, Erhard. *Wesen und Herkunft des "apodiktischen Rechts."* Neukirchen: Neukirchener Verlag, 1965.

Gevaryahu, Haim M. I. "Privathäuser als Versammlungsstätten von Meister und Jüngern." *ASTI* 12(1983)5–12.

Gevirtz, Stanley. "On Canaanite Rhetoric." *Orientalia* 42 (1973)162–77.

Gibson, John C. L., tr. *Canaanite Myths and Legends.* Edinburgh: T. & T. Clark, 1977.

Gilbert, Maurice. "Le discours de la Sagesse en Proverbes, 8." In *La Sagesse de l'Ancien Testament,* edited by M. Gilbert. Leuven: University Press, 1979, 202–18.

Ginzberg, Louis. *The Legends of the Jews,* 7 vols. Philadelphia: Jewish Publication Society, 1946–64.

Goebel, Franz M. *Jüdische Motive im märchenhaften Erzählgut.* Gleiwitz: Oberschlesische Volksstimme, 1932.

Goldberg, Arnold. *Untersuchungen über die Vorstellungen von der Schekhinah.* Berlin: de Gruyter, 1969.

Goldingay, John E. "Proverbs V and IX." *RB* 84(1977)80–93.

Gordon, Cyrus H. *The Common Background of Greek and Hebrew Civilizations.* New York: Norton, 1965.

Greeley, Andrew M. *The Mary Myth: On the Femininity of God.* New York: Seabury, 1977.

Guglielmi, Waltraud, "Personifikation." In *Lexikon der Ägyptologie,* vol. 4, edited by Wolfgang Helck et al. Wiesbaden: Harrassowitz, 1982, 978–87.

Gunkel, Hermann. *Zum religionsgeschichtlichen Verständnis des Neuen Testaments.* Göttingen: Vandenhoeck & Ruprecht, 1903.

Hallo, William W., and van Dijk, J. J. A. *The Exaltation of Inanna.* New Haven, CT: Yale University Press, 1968.

Haran, Menahem. "Book-Scrolls in Israel in Pre-Exilic Times." *JJS* 33(1982)161–73.

Haussig, Hans Wilhelm, ed. *Wörterbuch der Mythologie,* vol. 1:1. Stuttgart: Klett, 1965.

Hegel, Georg W. F. *Philosophie der Weltgeschichte,* 2d ed., vol. 2, edited by G. Lasson. Leipzig: Meiner, 1923.

Heimpel, Wolfgang. "A Catalog of Near Eastern Venus Deities." *Syro-Mesopotamian Studies* 4(1982)59–72.

Heinze, Richard. *Vom Geist des Römertums,* 3d ed. Darmstadt: Wissenschaftliche Buchgesellschaft, 1960.

Heller, Joseph. *God Knows* [A novel]. New York: Alfred Knopf, 1984.

Hengel, Martin. *Judentum und Hellenismus,* 2d. ed. Tübingen: J. C. B. Mohr, 1973.

Hennecke, Edgar, ed. *Neutestamentliche Apokryphen in deutscher Übersetzung,* 3d ed., edited by W. Schneemelcher, vol. 2. Tübingen: J. C. B. Mohr, 1964.

Herzog, Zeev. *The City-Gate in Eretz-Israel and its Neighboring Countries.* Tel Aviv: Institute of Archaeology, Tel-Aviv University, 1976 [Hebrew, Engl. summary].

Hölderlin, Friedrich. "Parallele zwischen Salomons Sprüchwörtern und Hesiods Werken und Tagen" (1790). In *Sämtliche Werke,* vol. 4/1, edited by Friedrich Beissner. Stuttgart: Cotta 1961, 176–88.

Horsley, Richard A. "Spiritual Marriage with Sophia." *Vigiliae Christianae* 33(1979)30–54.

Hrushka, B. "Das spätbabylonische Lehrgedicht *Inannas Erhöhung.*" *Archiv Orientální* 37(1969)473–522.

Humbert, Paul. "Eteindre la main. Note de lexicographie hébraïque." *VT* 12(1962)383–95.

Iser, Wolfgang. *The Act of Reading: A Theory of Aesthetic Response.* Baltimore: Johns Hopkins University Press, 1978.

Ismail, Kamil. *Die sozialökonomischen Verhältnisse der bäuerlichen Bevölkerung der Syrischen Arabischen Republik.* Berlin: Akademie-Verlag, 1975.

Jacobsen, J. "A propos de Proverbes VIII,22 à 31." *RHPhR* 9(1929)468–73.

Jax, Karl. *Die weibliche Schönheit in der griechischen Dichtung.* Innsbruck: Universitätsverlag Wagner, 1933.

Johnson, A. R. *The One and the Many in the Israelite Conception of God,* 2d ed. Cardiff: University of Wales Press, 1961.

Kant, Immanuel. *Werke,* vol. 1, edited by Wilhelm Weischedel. Darmstadt: Wissenschaftliche Buchgesellschaft, 1956.

Kayatz, Christa B. *Studien zu Proverbien 1–9.* Neukirchen: Neukirchener Verlag, 1966.

Keel, Othmar. *Die Weisheit spielt vor Gott: Ein ikonographischer Beitrag zur Deutung des meṣaḥāqät in Sprüche 8,30f.* Fribourg: Universitätsverlag, 1974.

―――. *The Symbolism of the Biblical World.* ET, T. J. Hallett. New York: Seabury, 1978.

Kern, Peter. *Trinität, Maria, Inkarnation: Studien zur Thematik der deutschen Dichtung des späten Mittelalters.* Berlin: E. Schmidt, 1971.

Kloppenborg, John S. "Isis and Sophia in the Book of Wisdom." *HTR* 75(1982)57–84.

Koch, Klaus. "Saddaj: Zum Verhältnis zwischen israelitischer Monolatrie und nordwestsemitischem Polytheismus." *VT* 26(1976)299–332.

―――. "Is There a Doctrine of Retribution in the Old Testament?" In

Theodicy in the Old Testament, edited by James L. Crenshaw. Philadelphia: Fortress Press, 1983, 57–87.

————. *The Prophets.* ET, M. Kohl, vol. 2. Philadelphia: Fortress, 1984.

Köhler, Ludwig. *Der hebräische Mensch.* Tübingen: J. C. B. Mohr, 1953.

Kraeling, C. H., and Adams, R. M., eds. *City Invincible: A Symposium on Urbanization and Cultural Development.* Chicago: University of Chicago Press, 1960.

Kraeling, Emil G. *The Brooklyn Museum Aramaic Papyri.* New Haven, CT: Yale University Press, 1953.

Kraus, F. R. "Das altbabylonische Königtum." In *Le palais et la royauté.* 19ième rencontre assyriologique internationale 1971. Paris: Geuthner, 1974, 235–61.

Küchler, Max. *Frühjüdische Weisheitstraditionen.* Fribourg: Universitätsverlag, 1979.

Labuschagne, C. J. "The Emphasizing Particle *gam* and Its Connotations." In *Studia Biblica et Semitica T. C. Vriezen Dedicata.* Wageningen: Veenman & Zonen, 1966, 193–203.

Lane, Edward William. *Manners and Customs of the Modern Egyptians.* Everyman's Library. London: Dent & Sons, 1954.

Landauer, Georg. *Palästina: 300 Bilder.* Munich: Meyer & Jessen, 1925.

Lang, Bernhard. *Die weisheitliche Lehrrede: Eine Untersuchung von Sprüchen 1–7.* Stuttgart: Kath. Bibelwerk, 1972.

————. "Schule und Unterricht im alten Israel." In *Wie wird man Prophet in Israel? Aufsätze.* Düsseldorf: Patmos, 1980, 104–19.

————. "The Yahweh-Alone Movement and the Making of Jewish Monotheism." In *Monotheism and the Prophetic Minority.* Sheffield: Almond Press, 1983a, 13–59.

————. "Ein babylonisches Motiv in Israel Schöpfungsmythologie." *BZ* 27(1983b)236–37.

Larcher, C. *Etudes sur le livre de la Sagesse.* Etudes bibliques. Paris: Gabalda, 1969.

Lausberg, Heinrich. *Handbuch der literarischen Rhetorik.* Munich: Hueber, 1960.

Leipoldt, Johannes, and Grundmann, Walter, eds. *Umwelt des Urchristentums,* vol. 2. Berlin: Evangelische Verlagsanstalt, 1967.

Lemaire, André. *Les écoles et la formation de la Bible dans l'ancien Israël.* Fribourg: Editions Universitaires, 1981.

————. "Sagesse et écoles." *VT* 34(1984)270–81.

Lewis, Ioan M. *Social Anthropology in Perspective.* Harmondsworth: Penguin, 1976.

Lichtenstein, M. "The Banquet Motifs in Keret and in Prov. 9." *JANES* 1 (1968/69)19–31.

186

Lichtheim, Miriam, tr. *Ancient Egyptian Literature,* vols. 1 and 2. Berkeley: University of California Press, 1973/76.

von Lilienfeld, Fairy. "Sophia—die Weiheit Gottes.Über die Visionen des W. Solowjew." *Una Sancta* 39(1984)113–29.

Lindblom, Johannes. "Det offentliga talet i det gamla Israel." In *Studier tilegnede Frants Buhl,* edited by J. C. Jacobsen. Copenhagen: V. Pios, 1925, 112–26.

Lindenberger, James M. *The Aramaic Proverbs of Ahiqar.* Baltimore: Johns Hopkins University Press, 1983.

Lohfink, Norbert et al. *Ich will euer Gott werden: Beispiele biblischen Redens von Gott.* Stuttgart: Kath. Bibelwerk, 1981.

Loretz, Oswald. "Ugaritische und hebräische Lexikographie (iii)." *UF* 14(1982)141–48.

Luckenbill, Daniel D. *Ancient Records of Assyria and Babylonia,* vol. 2. Chicago: University of Chicago Press, 1927.

Macholz, Christian G. "Zur Geschichte der Justizorganisation in Juda." *ZAW* 84(1972)314–40.

Mack, Burton L. *Logos und Sophia: Untersuchungen zur Weisheitstheologie im hellenistischen Judentum.* Göttingen: Vandenhoeck & Ruprecht, 1973.

MacRae, George W. "The Jewish Background of the Gnostic Sophia Myth." *Novum Testamentum* 12(1970)86–101.

McKane, William. *Proverbs: A New Approach.* London: SCM Press, 1970.

———. *Prophets and Wise Men,* 2d ed. London: SCM Press, 1983.

Marböck, Johann. "Gesetz und Weisheit." *BZ* 20(1976)1–21.

Mattingly, Harold. "Personifications." *The London Mercury* 19(1928/29) 159–65.

———. "The Roman *Virtues.*" *HTR* 30(1937)103–17.

———. *Roman Coins,* 2d ed. London: Methuen, 1960.

Mazar, Benjamin, ed. *The World History of the Jewish People,* vol 4:2. Jerusalem: Massada Press, 1979.

Meissner, Bruno. *Babylonien und Assyrien,* 2 vols. Heidelberg: Winter, 1920, 1925.

Mercerus, Joannes. *Commentarii in Salomonis Proverbia* [etc.]. Geneva: Vignon, 1573.

Mielke, Ursula. "Sapientia." In *Lexikon der christlichen Ikonographie,* vol. 4. Freiburg: Herder, 1972, 39–43.

Milton, John. *The Works,* vol. 15, edited by Frank A. Patterson. New York: Columbia University Press, 1933.

Moore, George F. *Judaism,* vol. 2. Cambridge, MA: Harvard University Press, 1927.

Mooren, Thomas. "Monothéisme coranique et anthropologie." *Anthropos* 76(1981)529–61.

Moran, William L. "The Ancient Near Eastern Background of the Love of God in Deuteronomy." *CBQ* 25(1963)77–87.

Morenz, Siegfried. *Religion und Geschichte des Alten Ägypten.* Weimar: H. Böhlau, 1975.

Nachtigal, J. C. C. "Über die Weisen-Versammlungen der Israeliten." *Eichhorn's Allgemeine Bibliothek der Biblischen Litteratur* 9(1799)379–451.

Neumann, Frederick. *Über das Lachen.* 'sGravenhage: Nijhoff, 1971.

Nickelsburg, George W. E., and Stone, Michael E. *Faith and Piety in Early Judaism: Texts and Documents.* Philadelphia: Fortress Press, 1983.

Niditch, Susan. "The Wronged Woman Righted: An Analysis of Genesis 38." *HTR* 72(1979)143–49.

Nigg, Walter. *Drei grosse Zeichen: Elias—Hiob—Sophia.* Olten: Walter Verlag, 1972.

Nilsson, Martin P. *Die hellenistische Schule.* Munich: Beck, 1955.

Oesterley, William O. E. *The Book of Proverbs.* London: Methuen, 1929.

Ott, Ludwig. *Grundriss der Dogmatik,* 7th ed. Freiburg: Herder, 1965.

Parker, Simon B. "Parallelism and Prosody in Ugaritic Narrative Verse." *UF* 6(1974)283–94.

Passioni dell'Acqua, Anna. "La Sapienza e in genere l'elemento intermedio tra Dio e il creato nelle versioni greche dell' Antico Testamento." *Ephemerides Liturgicae* 98(1984)97–147.

Perdue, Leo G. *Wisdom and Cult.* Missoula, MT.: Scholars Press, 1977.

Pfeifer, Gerhard. *Ursprung und Wesen der Hypostasenvorstellung im Judentum.* Stuttgart: Calwer Verlag, 1967.

Pfleger, Karl. *Die verwegenen Christozentriker.* Freiburg: Herder, 1964.

Plöger, Otto. *Sprüche Salomos* (Proverbia). Biblischer Kommentar Altes Testament. Neukirchen: Neukirchener Verlag, 1984.

Pope, Marvin H. *El in the Ugaritic Texts.* VTS 2. Leiden: Brill, 1955.

Porten, Bezalel. *Archives from Elephantine.* Berkeley: University of California Press, 1968.

Pötscher, W. "Personifikation." In *Der kleine Pauly. Lexikon der Antike,* vol. 4. Munich: Druckenmüller, 1972, 661–63.

Preminger, Alex, ed. *Princeton Encyclopedia of Poetry and Poetics,* enlarged ed. Princeton, NJ: Princeton University Press, 1975.

von Rad, Gerhard. *Wisdom in Israel.* Nashville, TN: Abingdon Press, 1972.

———. *Das erste Buch Mose, Genesis,* 10th ed. Das Alte Testament Deutsch. Göttingen: Vandenhoeck & Ruprecht, 1976.

188

Rankin, Oliver S. *Israel's Wisdom Literature.* Edinburgh: T. & T. Clark, 1936.

Renan, Ernest. *Oeuvres complètes,* vol. 6, edited by H. Psichari. Paris: Calmann-Lévy, 1953.

Renger, Johannes. *"isinnam epeshum:* Überlegungen zur Funktion des Festes in der Gesellschaft." In *Les fêtes en Mésopotamie.* Actes de la 17ième rencontre assyriologique internationale 1969. Ham-sur-Heure: Comité Belge de Recherches Historiques, 1970, 75–80.

Ringgren, Helmer. *Word and Wisdom: Studies in the Hypostatization of Divine Qualities and Functions in the Ancient Near East.* Lund: Ohlsson, 1947.

Robinson, Theodore H. "Anacrusis in Hebrew Poetry." In *Wesen und Werden des Alten Testaments. BZAW* 66. Berlin: Töpelmann, 1936, 37–40.

Rodríguez-Herranz, J. C. "La hipóstasis de la sabiduría en Prov. 8,22–31." *Miscelánea Comillas* 56(1972)25–64.

Röttger, Hermann. *Mal'ak Jahwe: Die Vorstellung von Gottes Boten im hebräischen Alten Testament.* Frankfurt: P. Lang, 1978.

van Roon, A. "The Relation Between Christ and the Wisdom of God According to Paul." *Novum Testamentum* 16(1974)207–39.

Rudolph, Kurt. "Sophia und Gnosis." In *Altes Testament—Frühjudentum—Gnosis,* edited by Karl-Wolfgang Tröger. Gütersloh: Gütersloher Verlagshaus G. Mohn, 1980, 221–37.

Rüger, Hans Peter. "*Amôn*—Pflegekind: Zur Auslegungsgeschichte von Prv 8:30a." In *Übersetzung und Deutung, A. R. Hulst dargebracht.* Nijkerk: Callenbuch, 1977, 154–63.

Sachs, Hans. *Dichtungen,* vol. 3, edited by A. von Keller. Tübingen: Litterarischer Verein, 1870.

Said, Edward W. *Orientalism.* New York: Vintage Books, 1979.

Sanders, James A. *The Psalms Scroll of Qumran Cave 11 (11QPsᵃ).* Discoveries in the Judaean Desert of Jordan, vol. 4. Oxford: Clarendon Press, 1965.

———. *Torah and Canon.* Philadelphia: Fortress Press, 1972.

Sartre, Jean-Paul. *Qu'est-ce que la littérature?* Paris: Gallimard, 1948.

Sayce, A. H. *The "Higher Criticism" and the Verdict of the Monuments,* 7th ed. London: SPCK, 1908.

Schechter, Salomon, ed. *Aboth de Rabbi Nathan.* London: Nutt, 1887.

Schechter, Solomon. *Aspects of Rabbinic Theology.* New York: Schocken, 1961.

Schencke, Wilhelm. *Die Chokma (Sophia) in der jüdischen Hypo-*

stasenspekulation. Videnskapsselskapets Skrifter, II. Hist.-filos. klasse 1912, no. 6. Kristiania: H. Dybwad, 1913.

Schiller, Gertrud. *Ikonographie der christlichen Kunst,* vol. 4/1. Gütersloh: Gütersloher Verlagshaus G. Mohn, 1976.

Schmid, Hans Heinrich. *Gerechtigkeit als Weltordnung.* Tübingen: J. C. B. Mohr, 1968.

————. *Altorientalische Welt in der alttestamentlichen Theologie.* Zürich: Theologischer Verlag, 1974.

Schmitt-Fiack, Renate. *Wise und Wisheit bei Eckhart, Tauler, Seuse und Ruusbroec.* Meisenheim: Hain, 1972.

Schneider, Karl. "Hetairai." In *Paulys Realenzyklopädie der classischen Altertumswissenschaft,* new. ed., vol. 8. Stuttgart: Druckenmüller, 1913, 1331–72.

Schott, Siegfried. *Altägyptische Liebeslieder.* Zürich: Artemis, 1950.

Schüssler Fiorenza, Elisabeth. *In Memory of Her: A Feminist Theological Reconstruction of Christian Origins.* New York: Crossroad, 1983.

Scott, Robert B. Y. *Proverbs.* The Anchor Bible. Garden City, NY: Doubleday, 1965.

von Selms, A. "Temporary Henotheism." In *Symbolae Biblicae et Mesopotamicae F.M.T. de Liagre Böhl.* Leiden: Brill, 1973, 341–48.

Seuse, Heinrich. *Deutsche mystische Schriften, aus dem Mittelhochdeutschen übertragen von G. Hofmann.* Düsseldorf: Patmos, 1966.

Sheppard, Gerald T. *Wisdom as a Hermeneutical Construct.* BZAW 151. Berlin: de Gruyter, 1980.

Shiloh, Y. "The Four-Room House—the Israelite Type-House?" *Eretz-Israel* 11(1973)277–85.

Sjöberg, Åke W. "The Old Babylonian Eduba." In *Sumerological Studies in Honor of T. Jacobsen,* edited by St. J. Lieberman. Chicago: University of Chicago Press, 1976, 159–79.

Skehan, Patrick W. "Structures in Poems on Wisdom: Proverbs 8 and Sirach 24." *CBQ* 41(1979)365–79.

Smith, Morton. *Palestinian Parties and Politics that Shaped the Old Testament.* New York: Columbia University Press, 1971.

————. "On the Differences Between the Culture of Israel and the Major Cultures of the Ancient Near East." *JANES* 5 (1973)389–95.

Smith, Sidney. "The Meaning of *goren*." *PEQ* 85(1953)42–45.

Speiser, E. A. *Oriental and Biblical Studies.* Philadelphia: University of Pennsylvania Press, 1967.

Stammler, Wolfgang. *Frau Welt: Eine mittelalterliche Allegorie.* Fribourg: Universitätsverlag, 1959.

190

Staudenmaier, Franz Anton. *Die Lehre von der Idee.* Giessen: B. C. Ferber, 1840.

Suggs, M. Jack. *Wisdom, Christology, and Law in Matthew's Gospel.* Cambridge, MA: Harvard University Press, 1970.

Teilhard de Chardin, Pierre. *Writings in Time of War.* ET, René Hague. London: Collins, 1968.

Trible, Phyllis. "Wisdom Builds a Poem: The Architecture of Proverbs 1:20–33." *JBL* 94(1975)509–18.

Tristram, Henry B. *Eastern Customs in Bible Lands.* London: Hodder & Stoughton, 1894.

Tufnell, Olga. *Lachish (Tell ed-Duweir),* vol. 3: text. London: Oxford University Press, 1953.

Vawter, Bruce. "Prov. 8:22: Wisdom and Creation." *JBL* 99(1980) 205–16.

Vogt, Ernst. "Einige hebräische Wortbedeutungen." *Biblica* 48 (1967) 57–74.

Weber, Ferdinand. *Jüdische Theologie auf Grund des Talmud und verwandter Schriften.* Leipzig: Dörfflin & Franke, 1897.

Weber, Max. *The Theory of Social and Economic Organization.* ET, A. H. Henderson and T. Parsons. New York: Oxford University Press, 1947.

van der Weiden, W. A. *Le livre des Proverbes: Notes philologiques.* Rome: Biblical Institute Press, 1970.

Westermann, Claus. "Die Begriffe für Fragen und Suchen im Alten Testament." In *Forschung am Alten Testament,* vol. 2. Munich: Chr. Kaiser, 1974, 162–90.

Westermarck, Edward. *The Belief in Spirits in Morocco.* Acta Acad. Aboensis, Humaniora 1:1. Åbo:Åbo Akademi, 1920.

Whedbee, J. William. *Isaiah and Wisdom.* Nashville, TN: Abingdon Press, 1971.

Whitley, Charles F. "The Hebrew Emphatic Particle L with Pronominal Suffixes." *JQR* 65(1974/75) 225–28.

Whybray, Roger N. *Wisdom in Proverbs.* London: SCM Press, 1965.

Wilckens, Ulrich. *Weisheit und Torheit: Eine exegetisch-religionsgeschichtliche Untersuchung zu 1 Kor. 1 und 2.* Tübingen: J. C. B. Mohr, 1959.

———. "Sophia etc." In *Theologisches Wörterbuch zum Neuen Testament,* vol. 7, edited by Gerhard Friedrich. Stuttgart: Kohlhammer, 1964, 497–529.

Wildeboer, Gerrit. *Die Sprüche.* Kurzer Hand-Commentar zum Alten Testament. Freiburg: J. C. B. Mohr, 1897.

Wilken, Robert L., ed. *Aspects of Wisdom in Judaism and Early Christianity.* Notre Dame, IN: University of Notre Dame Press, 1975.

Winnett, F. V. "Allah before Islam." *The Moslem World* 28(1938)239–48.

Winter, Urs. *Frau und Göttin, Exegetische und ikonographische Studien zum weiblichen Gottesbild im Alten Israel und in dessen Umwelt.* Fribourg: Universitätsverlag, 1983.

Wiseman, D. J. "Rahab of Jericho." *Tyndale House Bulletin* 14(1964)8–11.

Wolff, Hans Walter. *Anthropologie des Alten Testaments.* Munich: Kaiser, 1973.

Xenophon. *Memorabilia and Oeconomicus.* ET, E. C. Marchant. The Loeb Classical Library, Xenophon, vol. 4. Cambridge, MA: Harvard University Press, 1923.

Yadin, Yigael. *Hazor: The Rediscovery of a Great Citadel of the Bible.* New York: Random House, 1975.

Yee, Gale A. "An Analysis of Prov. 8:22–31 According to Style and Structure." *ZAW* 94(1982)58–66.

Zeilinger, Franz. *Der Erstgeborene der Schöpfung: Untersuchungen zur Formalstruktur und Theologie des Kolosserbriefes.* Wien: Herder, 1974.

Zevit, Ziony. "The Khirbet el-Qôm Inscription Mentioning a Goddess." *BASOR* 255(1984)39–47.